THE JOURNEYMAN

For Angela, my life

THE
JOURNEYMAN

MICHAEL MURRAY

MAINSTREAM
PUBLISHING

EDINBURGH AND LONDON

First published in Great Britain in 2002 by
MAINSTREAM PUBLISHING COMPANY (EDINBURGH) LTD
7 Albany Street
Edinburgh EH1 3UG

ISBN 1 84018 551 1

A catalogue record for this book is available from the British Library

Typeset in Allise and Berkeley
Printed and bound in Great Britain by
Butler & Tanner Ltd, Frome and London

ACKNOWLEDGEMENTS

Thanks are due in particular to Ian, my father-in-law, for reading and rereading my initial scribblings, helping to clarify my thoughts and for exposing the grossest of my errors. Thanks, too, to Angela, who had to decipher my handwriting when typing the manuscript.

CONTENTS

A QUESTION TO THE CREATOR

Now that you have roped off a circle for hungry men to live, fight and die in, why don't you come into it yourself and see how you do?

INTRODUCTION

There's a new heavyweight in town, the Olympic Gold Medalist Audley Harrison. I have read and heard that my name is at the top of the list of fighters he'll beat on his way to becoming a professional World Heavyweight champion. Although at 19 st, 260-70 lb, perhaps that should be World Heavyweight chump. His manager, Colin McMillan (a former boxer), has already begun nursing him up the ranks, spoon-feeding him deadbeats; the southern English way of developing boxers.

A boxer's knowledge cannot be had from ghosts and spirits, or verified by astrological calculations. It must come from the experience of combat. Inside the ring there is a struggle for respect that leads either to victory or defeat. The matchmaker's job is to find a broken and defeated fighter and ensure almost certain victory for the prospect. The men already beaten and broken are called 'bodies'. The men not yet beaten, but who are believed to be close, are called 'journeymen'. Even a great champion can become a journeyman. We are men willing to fight anyone, anywhere, and all we require is money and enough time to put on our shorts and glove-up. At a guess we make up about 40 per cent of professional fighters. Of the remainder, 45 per cent are bodies, 10 per cent are prospects and the remainder champions.

All fighters start out as prospects but what credit should we give to the baby-sat fighter for his courage when he is conquering men who have already lost? Real courage lies in turning adversity into advantage. Intelligence is of the essence in the boxing ring; it is what the fighter depends upon when making his every move. An intelligent journeyman waits for his prospect to expose a vulnerability that will eclipse his strengths. We are all dangerous and we can become champions at any time. Most of us are avoided in favour of the 'bodies'.

A fight with its complex of conditions is very much alive. Experience helps us learn to coordinate the various ingredients that constitute a fighter's world and to extract the most out of what we have. It is not simply a quest of discovering or of grasping an unchanging reality behind the shadows of appearance, but a profound and creative odyssey where the quality of the journey is itself the end. Sooner or later Harrison will have to meet a live opponent, someone who can fight. Then what?

When I look back in time, I realise my fighter within was shown to me by a child I can hardly recall. The same childhood has created other men, men whose heads my fists have learned to kiss. They fall at the feet of lost time. Through rain and light this life has come down to me. I tell my story in order to find a meaning. I continue to fight in fear of losing myself. The hours close in on me; my transparent body shows me its dreams still in motion and the mission I must fulfil. Time repeats itself, hour by hour, day by day. Runs repeat themselves, mile by mile, and my body and I manage to find a balance between family and work. Our time floods before our eyes, from cradle to grave in a flash. Pictures, some unidentifiable, are kept in bundles for the journey, for when we become grown, even though our fathers were never more than boys. After young minds have become sharpened by the fight to survive, our bravery is tested to the fullest. After we've thrown our youth into the water and mocked our young days, how can we accept the brief life that time in the end will take?

1

AN ENGLISH BOY IN PARADISE

Born in Preston, England, to Jamaican immigrants with nothing, I've spent many years trying to free myself from my fate. The umbilical cord that tied me to my background was cut with the sword of a samurai warrior a decade ago, and nothing remains. But there's still a voice that lives inside me, that manifests itself in my cells and floats through my body, a Jamaican chorus to remind me of what nothing is: 'You is a wot'lis piece a nut'ting, a empty ting, a empty space, wid all di ada wot'lis piece a nut'ting in a dis world.' But I have within me all the dreams of this world. My head is clear and I refuse to die accepting that fate.

My father was a joiner and my mother a factory and hospital worker. Both came to England during the *Windrush* era when this country needed skilled workers. They had great expectations. They sat on a big ship and watched England arrive. Their courage must have been great. But how did they feel? They never described it. I imagine it must have been an empty feeling, so much so that they were unable to paint a picture of it for me. I think of a feeling on the remote side of joy. Maybe you can paint it better and vary the way it appears to you but the picture would show solitary figures facing themselves in bewilderment, with empty mixtures of other memories and minds, perplexed and eroded by the absence of home. Paint it as it suits you best but paint a couple alone. The surroundings don't matter. How do people who arrive in a vision of their dream recover from the reality of that dream?

This nice boy from England with anchored hopes was dropped into poverty somewhere across a large expectant ocean. Dropped into a Jamaican dream by parents he hardly knew. The earliest memory I have is holding on to my mother's leg screaming, begging and pleading with her not to leave me. I held on until my arms were torn from their embrace. It felt like I was dragged from her womb and thrown away. My youth was spent beating straw mattresses, chopping wood, feeding chickens and goats and avoiding school.

In Jamaica we have a thing called 'in-case licks'. In-case licks are beatings for something you might do or might have done; in case you did or were going to do. No child admits to anything and therefore every child is beaten. I was held captive by my aunt's belt-buckle, scorpions, lizards and vultures, all of whom knew my fears well on dark Caribbean nights. My feet were soft and clung to the ground, glued there by bleeding wounds. My toes itched for shoes to wear.

But the sunlight danced on young faces. Birds awoke from sweet dreams to fly over rainbowed landscapes. Children of the sun played in a dreamtime with no knowledge of how short the seasons were. With hand-built canoes they rode the waves of sorrow, but the time of hurricanes was always around the corner. Ill-tempered winds brought roaring surf. The hurricanes would put on such a show that frightened children would abandon their boats on white sands. They'd run into shelters to watch at a safer distance, leaving everything to the flamboyant gusts whose rage could not be caged.

One of my lingering memories from Jamaica was witnessing a train crash and its aftermath. This event would transform itself into a recurring dream of mine over the years, where spirits were unbound from a mass of dark twisted iron that rode the steel tracks leading to who knows where. Many died. I saw their white bones standing up through their flesh. It made me wonder, at what time was this island a paradise? Even the rainbow was content to hide and was absent from the skies. Near the crash there was a tall tree which I climbed to the top of to get a better view. My eyes were level with telegraph poles and their sizzling wires that curved for miles into the beyond. The wires sagged with the weight of vultures licking their beaks, eyes on their lunch. The first thing I saw was a group of scavengers with naked feet, running from something they couldn't see. They were untamed and wild. Sensing danger, they ran with wallets and jewellery in their hands, jewellery that would not be missed. They ran, busily seeking refuge, somewhere they could lay low for now and hide away from the law. They were not dreams, these thieves without fortune. I had seen them mirroring themselves in shop windows. I had seen them furious on their knees dressed in rags, savage with sun-dyed locks flying over their shoulders. I had dreamt of them trembling in the thunder of battle while their wounds bled into the sand.

I would see these scavengers again during the 1981 riots across Britain. They ran from shop windows with three-piece suites, televisions, refrigerators and whatever else they could carry, as riot police cursed our futile rage at the Thatcher government's racist policies. With shields they drove through the hearts of the living wounded, disfiguring our minds with well rehearsed and well executed swings of their batons. We tried to burn the racism out of our neighbourhoods by burning ourselves down. Analyse that logic!

The mountain of metal extended to the Jamaican sky. My breath felt as if it had shortened but its to and fro rhythm kept my pulse strong. I was alone in the tree and mute. I couldn't measure with my young eyes the immensity of what I saw. There came the terrible motion of people running that made everything shake including my tree. These onlookers looked up to heaven distraught as if their eyes had never seen such horror and the pain that swelled right there seemed to eclipse heaven. But still they looked to the unknown in the sky for refuge even though they had no parachutes and would be flattened upon the fall back to earth. An earth they wanted to leave. To fly upwards to find what? There is nothing there.

As the sun prepared to sleep on that Caribbean day I climbed down from the tree and ran to my grandmother's house on William Street, in the slums of Spanish Town, Jamaica. It happened to be in the neighbourhood of the crash and some of my aunts also lived on the same street. My grandmother always talked endlessly to people she saw every day. She talked for hours, chin wagging, endlessly giggling. Round and round the same subjects, a tireless tongue jumping through hoops of fire, never satisfied, excessively gossiping. Merciless verbal whippings were given to the deserved and undeserved day and night and never a sign of fatigue. On this day, when I tried to interrupt, her cracking whip encouraged my retreat. She continued, the sound of her voice slightly louder but familiarly happy, eventually fizzling out and stopping.

She turned to me and asked, 'Wha, wha u warnt?'

To which I could only reply, 'I just saw a train crash.'

When I returned home to my aunt's I was greeted with a brass-knuckle belt. If she had been home she would have been aware of my absence and I wouldn't have been one of the usual suspects.

It is true that I've failed in most things but maybe most things are nothing but dreams, something on the inside. I served my apprenticeship and paid my dues. I came into this world with great intentions but all I found were people exactly the same as others, who were exactly the same as me. In my dreams there are a billion brains each thinking that they are distinct from one another. I know that history will not record even one of them, even if they are all comfortable in their certainties. If their aspirations elevate them, then let them be noble and proud and let them attain their dreams. This world will be conquered by those who dare. I am no longer waiting for someone to open the doors to my future. I believe in myself. I can open the doors to my own universe and walk through with the hope I have built and join in the fight for freedom along with all the other hearts and souls enslaved by nothingness.

As I said before, in Jamaica nobody owns up to anything. No one was home and no one did whatever the thing was that we all got beaten for. Nine times out of ten I had no idea why I was met at the front door by a belt buckle. For me a summer's day often ended like that. I imagined myself, while I lay awake waiting for my tears to dry, on the other side of the island where people played barefoot in warm water and took long peaceful naps under the banana trees with half-closed eyes. There the sea swayed gently back and forth and dolphins danced with the rhythms of the waves, while the sun looked at its own reflection in the calm, glorious waters. There the tourists came with red faces to take on rivers, to stretch themselves while birds sang along with reggae bands. They ate fruit and walked long hours in the cool evening air. They drank the sweet juice of coconuts freshly picked from palm trees. That's where I wanted to be as I watched the sun close its eyes on my nightmare.

Often during the night, woken by the belt, I jumped from my urine-soaked bed into a dream of terror, knees quivering. I was not alone. I shared a bed with my brother Lance. He was a bed-wetter. I begged him to own up, to look within himself rather than at me, but he was like a child in the womb, detached and inarticulate. When the world accuses a child of things that it has invented to torture them with, what choice have the young but to suffer while their thoughts lie helplessly within? There was no escaping my aunt's tyranny. It eventually defeated Lance. He became unrecognisable, tragic and foolish without a tongue. Now all that remains is the frightened face of an illiterate man, locked away in a high-rise flat in Preston.

My sister Yvonne lived with our grandmother, while sisters Dione and Denise stayed with another aunt. Their experiences of Jamaica were altogether better than ours. My aunt had two kids. Come to think of it, I never saw them hit. Lance and I took their beatings for them, no matter what they did. I stood firm and violence lost, but I was always recaptured by violent hands and so consented to my cousins' deeds. Violence alone opens the head from which blood flows freely. Lance broke under the beatings but I would learn to use that childhood hurt for new rewards later on in life. At the time I forgot that one day I was supposed to be rescued alive, so I stood and cursed the ones who left me there for so long, drowning in a bed of urine.

The other things I learnt in Jamaica were the unspoken rules on the streets of Spanish Town. There no warning shot would be heard. The trigger would be pulled. Brains would disperse. Crowds would hover to see a child's face pressed against the pavement while maintaining a safe distance, just close enough to satisfy their morbid curiosities.

Once I saw a man cut down. He was a great big man from the end of my street. First there was the sound of a gun, a great loud sound followed by the falling of his body. A car crashed into a tree at the side of the road, its driver startled by the gunshot. There was a moment's silence, which got louder and louder as people began to arrive and talk about what had happened. I remember the shooting because it was the day after my ninth birthday. I remember running up to the body, which was lying next to a large rat whose entrails were hanging out. I remember thinking, 'How did the rat die? What did he do wrong to be dead in the mud, mutilated with all his guts spilt?' It began to rain, despite a clear sky without a cloud in sight. An ambulance came and took the big man away, a tow-truck took the car, and the people carried on about their business. My sadness was for a lonely dead rat hated by the world. I often think about it. It was a sad moment. He's gone now but my heart still beats for the rat the sky cried for, a godforsaken thing alive or dead.

Days, weeks, months, years in captivity. When I left the weight of feeling could not be carried away by my journey nor could it bring me closer to anyone. The bright solitary moon was ready to set as I cast one last glance behind. The distance tried to appear as something small but proved itself endless. I remember the land beneath the sky. The coastline of dim beaches in white sand stretching indistinctly all the way to England, all the way to where my reason began and ended. How could geography cancel these years of experience?

2

THE REUNION

I was ten when I came back to England and reunited with my parents but the distance remained. My family life seemed like an explosion on a gentle battleground. Here self-pitying adults demanded a different world and a better life, a complete comprehension of both, immediately. Little by little my father began to leave my mother. They grew tired of the many soundless battles of eyes behind the closed doors of their relationship; a recurring defeat of communication, then the empty space, the silent end to time. He was always afraid to reopen talks. Her incorruptible matter was like a tree that grew up durable to all nature's elements, lying in a soundless bed of earth with its back to the wind. After years of the loveless suspension of a marriage, they cared little what impression they were making on their children. It was just about them.

Then came a death, a funeral event. The unchaining of my grandmother's soul to exist beyond a voiceless and weary world. Drained of blood, empty of sky, an island of mourning, wounded without a moon, without the mouth that death closed forever. As I passed by my mother's bedroom I looked in through the open door. She had the window open. The sun was out and a warm breeze blew about the room empty of everything except her mother's memory and the marital bed shared uncomfortably between strangers. How much history was coiled up under her black skin like an unborn baby waiting to emerge? How empty did she feel with not a single achievement to boast about? She had packed a suitcase and was sitting on the edge of her bed. She poured a drink from a half-empty bottle of rum and swallowed every drop.

Without going into the room, I said, 'Are you leaving now?'

She never answered, just sat there. She went out of the front door with wet eyelids and a suitcase filled with ash and dust to cover the bitter earth. My brother, sisters and I were left behind with our father. The sky immediately became starless and vast, home to a child's dark thoughts. My father closed the door behind him and created more darkness. He left us to fend for ourselves without food, with only our beating hearts in the palms of our outstretched hands. I had to live outside of the law, my anonymous identity moving in silence, accountable only to the rules of hunger.

I was 12 when my father looked up at me through my bedroom window. I saw his eyes. They weren't full of shame, as I would have expected, but a strange kind of pride. It was a summer night. My mother was still overseas burying her own mother in a cold Jamaican grave. The roads were empty and my brother and sisters were asleep. He entered the front door and I heard footsteps climbing the stairs. That was the night a father lost the son he had helped give birth to. He somehow found the courage to rip out my heart. I understood that he made this sacrifice willingly, because it didn't matter what we thought. How much could he love his family with a whore's breasts in his hands and her fingers masturbating him until his seed was spent over my mother's bed?

After that night we were never together again as a family. He drove the woman to some corner of the world, came back and went to sleep, unaware that I'd crept outside my bedroom and seen him inside his blonde dream through a half-opened door. She was a white-faced home wrecker. That must have been his taste. If he had known I was there that night, would it have mattered? He left us for his blonde woman and drove off into the sunset but it wasn't happy ever after. Eventually everyone began to desert him, even his blonde illusion. By then it was too late to do right.

I haven't seen my father for years but recently I had a dream so vivid it seemed more than just a dream. In it I met my father and his complexion was rather pale. He said that he had lost his soul. His blood was cold and he wanted to know if he was dead. It seemed he had blotted out the pain of his reality, trying to hide in ignorance of the world in which he belonged. He explained that he felt like the pawn of someone who had fixed in advance omnipresent laws that sealed him into life. I explained to him that there are limits to all things and I asked him to whom he was saying goodbye. He was free from the human body with all its weakness in which he had walked on earth. But his shadow began to regret the illusion of its death. He was defeated by the treachery of his own infidelity. He'd used up his years. He had played emotional games with both my mother and the other woman. The power that preordained his destiny was as inevitable as a waterfall tumbling over a precipice. His universe was a dream of time, doomed to enter the darkness that expected it, once he had reached the limit of his life on earth.

He had the bitterness of a man who had looked long and hard at the lonely moon. He was a man who revolved in a circle, the centre of which oppressed him with loneliness, darkness, danger and the threat of defeat. Every act came back to haunt him in minute detail. I didn't know if he could be rescued from this empty circuit, but I know that this rotating night had sat him down in a corner on the outskirts of time, made him a remote shadow, unbroken by light. But no one cares about an empty space or a single-minded fool confronting his nameless fear. In his mind eternity kept on recurring in an endless, revolving memory of his flesh. Time will consider his vanity amongst men before transforming him into dust. A light will peer into his soul with no consideration for his privacy and discover every fault. It will judge without end in a night that will never be day.

Didn't he bring failure on himself with his own hand? Weren't his ideas and behaviour doomed to failure? Now what's left of tenderness and compassion are indecipherable. His soul bore witness to the dishonour of my mother. Perhaps he contrived his failure from the image he chose for himself. His flesh once weighed heavy on this earth. His eyes once looked into eyes that looked back with affection, but he lived an unfaithful past that celebrated lust and adulterous banquets with a naked woman. He was unable to make a deal with his fate to stop the memories that wouldn't leave him.

Here at the end of his dream, at the end of the universe, an endless search had begun for him. Here a man's cry could die a lonely death. Here, too, are a billion lost souls that never show themselves. They harmonise with the memories of half-forgotten melodies. Here the relationship between man and woman is so misunderstood that it is swept aside with forgotten time.

At the end of my dream, the wisdom of life unfolded around me and all I had seen of my father's life was obliterated. He was now cut off from me, frozen into a horrible type of deformity. For me he's the living dead. He will one day look back with anxious desire only to find that space has been divided by his existence. I mourned him in his chains, my pity taking death's image. In my eyes he is dead, separated from my vision. For my children he has never existed. When my mother came back from my siblings in Jamaica I saw only her grief, her falling tears. But can a father's ghost see his family crying and not cry himself? He had a new world to inherit, a world to receive his spirit. For me death poured sleep on his memory. It took an immortal day and replaced it with an eternal night.

The heart feels and understands more than the mind knows. My mother loved my father but was ashamed of it. Her soul floated in wonder, sought after rum to comfort her on a bed of water that reflected her dissolution. She followed her charted course, obedient to the irresistible currents. She had obeyed a violent marriage without protection. My father's rage rolled the waves of his jealous waters around her. She lay, pissed each night, floating amidst secret tears. The voice that abandoned her still echoed on her shores beneath the setting sun. She thought I couldn't see, thought my senses had shut me off from her and enclosed my young mind within a narrow circle, but she was wrong. My heart wouldn't sink into her abyss, or erase itself; wouldn't fall from life along with the father I reminded her of. In the morning she would wake with fresh tears and the days would be silent, but she always saw her image reflected in loving eyes.

3

SELF-EDUCATED

At school I never gained much education, proving myself to be the model dreamer. Yet every day I'd turn up wishful for knowledge, watching those who topped the class and gained everything school had to offer. I remember my friends numbered many more, but they too were lost in a daydream. If I were to see those old school friends again in passing they'd be nothing to my eyes but lost faces, shadows from a life dreamt while a schoolboy slept.

For me, school turned into a battle for motivation. Words remained unseen and unlearnt. My hand carried no ink stains. Sport was a seductive distraction compared to books and music, a delicious diversion from work. It was easy to succumb to PE's charm. I was also fascinated by literature and philosophy but they were subjects jealously guarded by an unforgiving hand, a teacher who carried within him his own ignorant pain. I can now say to that hand in a most simplistic way: 'The earth is made up of atoms, plants and animals, plus humans, despite their colour. If we are all formed from the same atoms, then without contradiction we must be formed by the same hand. It is a teacher's responsibility to see that and explain it to his pupils.'

I loved sports and PE. I played on all the teams – football, cricket, table tennis, badminton, volleyball, basketball and cross-country running. You can always count on the passion of sport to comfort the ruthless and their competitiveness but that comfort was short-lived and came to an end when I was called a nigger on the basketball court during a tournament against other schools. The referee turned a blind eye and I retaliated with my fists as if I had never learnt how to speak without hands. Those fists had their own dark reasons for exploding upon a boy's soul. I knew it was too late to take it back. They should've known that they explained the pain of a boy's life in their own silent way. I tried to control a volcano that had been rumbling between the cradle and that explosive moment, but I could not. Something told me to close my hands and make a fist. Pain and the boy met in an eruption of anger. I had intelligence, but, like many children, I used my fists until I was taught how to use my brains.

In an effort to stop my world from spinning the teacher imposed a year's ban from all sporting activities in school. My eyes overflowed with tears, which ran down unrepressed. I had sufficient enough comprehension to understand that the school was trying to stifle my spirit by hitting me where it hurt. Yes I was wrong, yes I was rough and yes I was no angel, but I was a child. Only very wise pupils turn up to school to learn what teachers have to teach them of time.

What if my wandering clan had given me one of those rich white bodies to be born in? I could have claimed their borrowed ancestry, embraced the longings and learning of their homes. Maybe I could have spelled my name right. But would I still have the appetite and rage, as well as my guilty self-contempt? Would I have remained at the dumb mouth of a cave shivering like a dog beneath the thunder, disposable trash to the passing eye? Born but never native here, this was the place I claimed. I lost and found my living history on England's changeable streets. I belonged with the unbelonging in a world of second-generation strangers. If I could have one wish to put the world in order, that wish would be that I could rid the world of hate.

Though I had a Jamaican accent I spoke in English. The shadow of my English teacher (whose name I don't remember) stood over me. Despite his civility, he seemed to enjoy baiting me and exposing my inability to read. Even as a child I could see it in his eyes, and it caused me to both hate and fear him. I would have thought an adult would have been aware of this, and that he would have tried instead to view his pupil with compassion, encouraging the child's halting words. 'Sit down, Murray' he would rage for the amusement of the class. I dealt with my classmates in the playground but in the classroom I felt mute and stupid. But I never bowed down to weep.

My time in Jamaica had cost me in terms of education. Absence from school had meant that I had never learnt how to read the books that were there. The sun and the ocean took my attention and when my spirit crossed the waters once again I was an illiterate young man about to attend high school in Preston. But consider my choices on a Caribbean island: school or the beach. Which would you have chosen? My thoughts had sound but spoke without words.

As humans we are sometimes afraid of ourselves and hide in ignorance. There was nothing mysterious about the books I had chosen not to understand, but all the same my incomprehension led me to fear them. Still I stood up to read, throwing a boy's spirit onto the classroom floor to tremble before the pale feet of my English teacher. He stamped on that little black boy like he was a cockroach. All flesh is born to the earth equally but even tamed animals will scent blood and their appetite can be seen as a carnivorous glare within their restless eyes. Such people's passions and emotions suddenly change everything and throw our nature back at us until we tear each other apart.

Soon after, for reasons unknown to me, this teacher's career was ended. The school gates were unlocked as he was escorted from the premises and his desk was cleared. But before he left he had turned his friend against me: my music teacher was to behave in the same way towards me. So, like a developing young warrior, I hung around the back of his classroom while my mind meditated. I saw the method by which ignorance is transmitted from generation to generation. There we were, receivers of knowledge, occupying our desks. There they were, the teachers who took the form of wise men, telling us how to exist in this world, all the while living in chains themselves. I didn't learn history, I learnt his-story. At times it felt like I was sitting, somehow suspended by a rope over an infinite abyss, my feet dangling into the deep beneath me. I wanted to speak but knew that if I did the rope that held me would be cut and I would fall into a vast web of hungry crawling spiders searching for their prey. If I questioned I knew I'd be thrown out of the lessons. So in my mind I answered, whilst in reality I lowered my eyes without saying a word, watching and listening. I felt like we had to ask, 'Permission to breathe, sir?'

There was a boy at school called David, who tried to go forward but no matter how hard he tried he just couldn't and so he was always forced to begin again. Adolescent inhibitions, fixed ideas and a scared mind blocked his way.

His mind had been branded with images of crucifixes, engulfed by wonder and curiosity. School always found him punctual and arriving without fanfare, generally in silent grey. He had a large mouth and fiercely repressed teeth that could not be seen. We pretended not to notice him and continued with our work. Our conversations of daily life were turned into silent whispers in his head; they filed away at his nerves, made him feel unsure of himself. His mind was busy with our talk of him, regardless of whether it was real or imagined.

One day after school, I started asking him about his beliefs, trying to catch him out with logic. 'If a firm persuasion of a thing is believed would that make it true?' Then I said, 'Answer this. God is said to have, through vain labour, created man in his own image, but I'd like to know how one image absorbs another. Isn't there an infinite number of images each made from the same earthly substance? So why isn't a monkey or a dog in God's image? Does an image claim the credit for the labour of its own images? Is it really man in God's image or simply God in man's?'

My words hung over his head. The questioned scared him into an irrational, violent retaliation against me; it was as if my reasoning threatened to cut the cord of hereditary beliefs which tied him to his mother.

I had a thirst for knowledge that consumed inside so I couldn't understand why he attacked me. I was seized in a whirlwind of rage and adrenaline, living pain that created enormous energy. In conflict humans grow apart then separate, leaving behind bitter fragments of life. The fight began to accumulate in me and swallowed everything, like distance and time, at the moment of his assault. He was strong and with a breathless, silent precision he blurred my horizon with a kick, a kick that landed against my face. It felt as sharp as a needle, and out of his mouth came a steady stream of profanity. I eluded every word. They could cause no pain. He threw another kick with the other leg and became entangled. I had not much fighting experience. I was only 14 or 15 years old and what I knew about fights didn't add up to much. I was shocked to feel a foot in my face. It disturbed the surface of my being, my equilibrium. He was a dangerous enemy. He said nothing, asked nothing and left behind only darkness and fear, yet he was only 15. He threw me to the ground and stepped back, one foot forward ready to kick me again. I stood up by instinct and my, as yet undiscovered, hands rose and shattered his jaw like crystal before he had time to raise his leg. He fell to the floor with a thud. A thud that neighbours heard through their walls. They came running, waving their hands up in the air, upset at the sight set before them. I walked away. I was suspended from school, excluded. My opinions were unalterable; my ignorance imposed on me. Lacking the ability to communicate my ideas had clearly lost me so much time. I carried a monkey on my back and grew vain believing that I was more intelligent than the monkey.

The fighter came next. My story had already begun. I dictated my words with hands and assumed my own power, however obscure or solitary. I unfolded my own vision, however shadowy or abstract. It appeared that I had won change in the battle's unseen aftermath. Silent passions contemplated and occupied themselves in unseen torment, stretched out across the cold world, frozen by an inner voice of terror.

I went home and said, 'Listen! Guess what happened today?'

My mother replied, 'I'm not interested. Go and play.'

Then a neighbour complained, 'Your son beat my son up today. What are you going to do about it?'

My mother said, 'Well, aren't boys always like that? Your son probably started it!'

'That's not true, you're wrong. Not my boy. Your son was like a vicious animal.'

'I know your type.'

'What type? Me?'

Then the neighbours told their stories of how I lived amongst them, and how they heard my father shouting and throwing his weight around, and my mother crying. Only this time it wasn't my father. By now my mother had drifted from one abusive relationship to another.

'Why don't you grow up and stay out of trouble?' she would ask. 'It's time you started listening.' The fighter had to come next. There was no way out of it.

I fed on the heads of bullies, dressed in clothes handed down from friends of the family. But I was born proud and raised tough, fearing no man. I became the terror of the streets. Where I walked bullies stepped aside. I began to enjoy a fight. What did it matter? A hateful mirror showed me every day my black face in a country indifferent to me.

4

ZEN

My friend David, the son of Dominican immigrants, lived across the road from me. After the fight we'd had at school we became very good friends. I was impressed with the way he fought with his legs. He could use them as well as some people use their hands. He introduced me to Thai Boxing. I introduced him to jazz. He took up the saxophone and became a jazz musician, though he was still afflicted by a martial arts bug that fed his life. For a time it became a passion with me also. When my soul slept, Bruce Lee appeared to me and told me that if the sun and moon doubted themselves they'd go out.

David and I travelled to Manchester every Saturday to train with Master Toddy, a Zen Buddhist from Thailand who had just arrived in England. He taught Thai Boxing in Piccadilly. Thai Boxing is an ancient martial art employing kicks, knees, elbows and punching. Within the ring there are definite rules. As in boxing, punches must be above the waist. But rabbit punches to the back of the head, holding and hitting, headbutting, elbows, backhands, wrestling, throwing the opponent to the ground; these are all within the rules. Our whole bodies became proud weapons. We sharpened our shinbones against trees, removing the flesh and killing the nerves, until leg-bones hardened through to the marrow. What else could pain do that hadn't already been done? While training, I had four fights that lasted a total of six rounds and never once felt a need to kick. I knocked them all out with my hands.

Master Toddy gave me my first book, *Zen and the Art of Archery* and told me to read it. I still carry that book in my memory. One particularly valuable lesson concerned visualising success: a master challenges warriors to shoot a pigeon through the eye from a great distance; the one who succeeded was the one who could only see the eye of the pigeon.

The book was meant to sort out the mess within my daily existence. A focus lesson to render the mess into something manageable. I understand that now. The wise never lose so much time as when they submit to learn from fools. The street taught me another lesson: a tiger provides for himself. I would know what was enough when I knew what was more than enough.

Walking down the street one Saturday night I surprised three bullies beating up a young black mate. I broke their noses, bloodied their heads and blackened their eyes. Their larger number was not a substitute for a big heart. Several police cars went by without seeing anything. I learned to fight on the streets. I liked the surge of adrenaline that flooded my flesh through my veins, travelling my body like a car down a motorway. A glance could stop an opponent with fear. My thoughts hid behind uncompromising dreams, which swam in my eyes and rippled over my abdominal centre. I could stop a man with hands and feet of water, raining on his exposed bones.

Time seemed to stretch out indefinitely, jumping from one fight to another. The fighting turned the world into something real, not a dream but something tangible. But this was to come to a stop one evening as I was walking home. I felt a shooting pain in my back. It came from a baseball bat. Pain passed through my nerves and shot to a million branches around my body. Fear shot through a nervous brain down into my heart. I swallowed air through struggling nostrils. Then my assailant's words articulated themselves from the depths of his eternal loneliness and set themselves free: 'Who the fuck do you think you are?'

I unfolded his words and heard my mind's eternal groans. Trembling, my thoughts held newborn terror. I knew nothing of words. My mind better contemplated conflict with a terrible monster. Pain is pain. Blood is red. When the opportunity is presented to free oneself from the chains held by a faceless master, the soul clenches its fists and that image of mystery is lost in hand-to-hand combat. I had no real recollection of what followed.

I was 16 and mean, a lethal weapon. I walked in fierce anguish with an unquenchable thirst. My heart beat in an obscure separation of body and soul. I was a child cursing the fathomless void beneath my formless and unmeasured feet. I was talked about in town but I didn't care. Following the incident with the baseball bat, a story went around about a man found face down, unconscious in his own blood and vomit. The police were called and then came a night in jail. Though I had defended myself against a notorious bully, a so-called hard man, my brain ached in the merciless silent night. When wearied I tried to stay awake, confused by the memory, worried by the silence. But nothing happened.

I woke to the sound of keys and I understood that for a long time when I'd had a choice I'd chosen the company of corrupt men. Always the vicious, difficult, company of villains. This way of thinking happened when hunger lasted for too many days, but at least in jail I got fed. After that everyone was careful not to get too close, because although I was young and quiet I could still drop you with a single punch, just as I had that man. I fought hard to raise myself from the bottom of the world, where fighters were bred. I rolled up my sleeves knowing that I was not a mistake and that one day the living quality of my mind would stand out.

5

A DEAD MARINE

We inhabit our own world, a world often too small for dreamers like you and I. My dream world began to fade when I entered adulthood. The adult life often forces us dreamers to search for new visions and hopes. I wanted to grow up to be a musician but my shoulders grew strong. One day I closed my eyes (I don't remember when exactly) and my dream faded into something else. When I opened my eyes again, I found myself between the ropes with a pair of gloves on, obeying the Queensberry Rules: already an expert at putting your lights out.

I was hungry for music as a young man. I found my way through record shops everywhere. While my friends were out drinking and pulling girls I stayed home with my collection of rare Blue Notes.

One day as I walked down a city street I heard a sound of wonderful colour, a sound I had never heard before, with shades of blue and green. I searched for its origin and once I discovered where it was coming from I ran into the shop and asked the assistant what was playing. 'Miles Davis, *Kind of Blue*,' she said. I bought a copy and took it home to add to the rest of my collection. I played that record day and night, until its melodies echoed in my head even while I slept. Miles Davis was the sound discovered by the bird of night, a sound that spreads its wings through miles of sky with the aid of a trumpet: a three-valve living thing that sings. Davis blew precious notes, notes of love carefully balanced between melody and harmony. A single phrase is enough to sink us in the middle of sound, a sound only interrupted by dynamic silences and accompanied by great rhythm. He left his legacy and went into the darkness, eyes wide open, leaping miles ahead into rivers of sound, endless waters of music.

There was no time to spare. I had to play the trumpet. My soul examined itself and decided it couldn't live without this voice. I had no choice. Then a brick wall: trumpets were too expensive for a single mother of five, with a mortgage, living on a nurse's wage. I knew not to ask. Santa had scratched my name off his gift list a long time ago. I put my head together with my friend Fergi. We faced the challenge together. How could we raise the money I needed to buy a trumpet? By chance we found the answer when I sold a bike to a cycling-shop owner who asked no questions. So in our minds we had our answer. We became the best bike thieves in England. No bicycle was safe. If you locked it up, we took the wheels. If you locked up the wheels, we took the frame. If you locked up the handlebars, we took the seat, and so on. The shop owner always bought from us without saying a word. It didn't take long before I had the money to buy myself a very nice Yamaha trumpet. I've never stolen since.

You could have stopped the world in space and taken away the human race. There was nothing else I needed that could have made me feel better than my trumpet. It was a beautiful love affair. I slept with my Yamaha on my pillow and practised day and night. I prayed to the trumpet god who looked like a cross between Louis Armstrong and Miles Davis.

If you ask what jazz is, I'd tell you to listen to your heart beating with nothing else to do. When Miles plays you hear the wind moving through his trumpet. Sit quietly and hear sounds come without hurry, just a breath, not so strong but strong enough. Listen to him and hold on to the memory of that sound. Feel his rhythm caress your eardrums. Feel him buzz around your head as sweet as a whisper. Close your eyes and let him move down to your feet and you'll say you've never heard anything like it. Sounds that are so perfectly calm, perfectly amazing.

Our youth diverged so much so that minutes, hours, days, months and years were just journeys around a circle of overlapping dreams. We put on the armoured suits of our fantasies, which allowed us to do so many dangerous things. As young boys we shoplifted and stole cars. The daughters of English kings ruled us with their language of free love. We took them but saw through their deceptions and moved on. We got involved in punch-ups in nightclubs and on football grounds. After arriving at Preston train station, visiting football supporters would be given police escorts to the North End football ground. But we cut off all the exits in and out of town, dividing into small groups of fighters. Then a dozen or so volunteers would run into the crowd and break it up with flashing hands, feet, heads, elbows, action and passion. The waiting groups would then pick off the opposition as they ran in confusion still looking for a fight. This strategy worked particularly well against the National Front invasions of the time. This was our turf. We tried to follow dreams, tried to reach out for something to hold onto. But camouflage hid the swiftest movements before taking life and dissolving back into the night. How stupidly we fought against our fate.

Fergi joined the Marines. He's dead now. I loved him like a brother. Franklyn Ferguson, Fergi, was the son of Trinidad immigrants who then lived in Preston, England. He was strong and well-built and was the first friend I made on my return home from Jamaica. We were close friends, like family, throughout high school. I loved his parents. Throughout his childhood he worshipped his elder brother, a man-mountain about 7 ft, a Marine MP (Military Police). He sold Franklyn endless stories that shaped his young mind. Our childhood passed away but his passion for the army remained part of his dreams. I remember his telling me that he'd dreamt about a fight, of lifting an Argentine off his feet with a knife and throwing him down like a sack of bones, seeing the soldier agonise and die before crouching down over the body to clean his blade. The army was like an injected drug to Fergi and war hadn't even begun. Day after day he lay in dark, damp soil in preparation for warfare. Without risk he ran long miles in full kit, encountering cold winds, and all the while his parting lips drank peace.

Franklyn the soldier came home on leave when we were 19. I thought I recognised him but he'd lost his features. His image had faded. I saw him but I no longer knew for sure whether it was him. He had lost himself to his army identity and allowed himself to be led by army restrictions. He just seemed indifferent and docile. People treated him differently, not because of him but rather for the uniform he wore. He walked towards me holding out his right hand to shake mine. We chatted for awhile in the street where we once played. He began by telling me that he'd taken part in four boxing bouts and had won them all by knockout. He had always been a good athlete. A group of guys anxiously waited for him in a Ford Transit van. He went on to speak about his wish to fight in the Falkland Isles conflict.

I asked him, 'Why?'

He said, 'Because I want to fight for my country.'

Again I asked him, 'What if your country is wrong, and those islands belong to Argentina?'

'I know your way of thinking,' he answered. 'War scares you.'

'Scared?' I replied.

'Leave the fighting to me,' he remarked with a grin.

'You know it's not fear.'

But right there I understood how different our destinies were. His was to wage war on the other side of the world and mine was music (at the time). I'd been offered a few conditional places in several music colleges, all depending on exam results. We could not see eye to eye. He kept on repeating that the Marines were giving him a great life, as if trying to draw me into his world. He paid no attention to anything I said. That was the last time we spoke. Someone called out to him from the van. We said our farewells in the street and he walked to the waiting vehicle and waved goodbye. It was an ordinary afternoon. We would never see each other again.

Six months later he was dead. It was a bizarre death that I didn't know how to handle back then, one I've never been able to forget. I look at his memory and now I see behind his last goodbye an infinite separation. Time took without anger a most heroic soul. His death was faithful to secret Marine laws. They called it a training accident at their German base. He now sleeps and dreams, unknown to the country he was willing to kill and die for. The events of life are so far-reaching that when one man dies, though it may cause wonder it is easy to forget that something or an infinite number of things die in every death. The dream of one man is just a part of the memory of all. What candle can I hold for a dead soldier? A boy whose eyes smiled with goodbye. His was a short life that today seems even shorter. Fergi was given just long enough to help himself to nothing more than air. Though soldiers are not blind to the realities of their situation, my soul still grieves for doomed youth.

We trained hard to be fighters. We ran against roaring winds along the side of rivers, more alive then than I realised. But life was still ahead. Insistent hands that thought only they knew the limits. They could scream, strike and paralyse then lower themselves from sight into the comfort of large pockets. We understood little of consequences, blindly stepping on whoever or whatever got in the way of our growth. Shadows boxed against unprepared shadows in the moments our life had trained us for. Every life is a mystery, even yours. Some people will tell you that suffering is good for your character. You're free to believe anything you like. If you ask me if I'd live it all again, making the same unforgivable mistakes, given half a chance. Yes, I would.

I wonder if there were other paths for young uneducated boys?

Well, there was always the army. But don't they want young men from good families with no criminal record? At one point I wanted to be a soldier. I could run like a cheetah to the horizon and back. My huge hands could tear men to pieces if they got in my way. But the business of being a soldier, crawling around in the dirt like a dog with no real engagement with an enemy – that, I couldn't do.

In the end I was forced to make a decision of my own about my career. I took up boxing, following the tradition in England, the birthplace of the modern fighter. I chose and my mother told me they'd chew me up and spit me out and never bother to examine the wounds where the teeth-marks were deepest. How could she have observed the broken crust of her sister's love or the buckled, pierced skin of her child's being? She never knew that being chewed and spat out had already become my life. I don't think that if she had witnessed me shedding men's blood I would have been saved from her doubt. Defeat was the only thing she could see for me.

I crossed an ocean of experience with raging fists. The trails of blood that fed rational needs were long. The stains wash away easily from fabric, using the right soap of course, but blood spilled brands its memory on the mind. I fought against giant waves with the thunder of persistent hands. I met lightning with two-handed combinations and found the power to deliver myself from the frequent storms. I'd spent my childhood riding furious waves, through cold darkness with blackened eyes. The power of those predetermined waves was always evident and seemed to be directed towards me. Strength would never have been enough. But the courage to fight is what gives the heart its rhythm and beats purpose into a fighter's life.

6

SINGLE PARENT

At age 17, I fell in love. Alison, whose face was pale, tried the puzzle of my prison and almost solved it with a kiss. But her parents rejected this poor black male with no prospects, who could never have been good enough for their daughter. She'd been privately educated in a Hertfordshire ballet school and was obviously going places. To them a stranger would always be strange. They would always make him feel uncomfortable for whatever reason. Maybe being separate or uniquely different had some part to play in it? But I believe it was simply pigment: nappy hair; big lips; having the wrong shade for the time of day. For that they could never be one with the stranger. Never accept his gods or his beliefs. Even if I'd become another being and they'd become another, then those two beings would have been strangers. Would a stranger only accept a stranger with a bigger gun than his own? Or, in their case, more wealth? Would that gun or wealth be the only reason for a peaceful acceptance? Why had the kissing stopped? What cruel, obscure instinct moved her pale hands, subtly pushing me away? I looked into her cold white eyes and asked her to speak. She didn't say a word. I saw grief, misunderstanding and the racist beliefs of her parents dividing us in the dark. There was a distinct silence deep within her. Silence and the lack of intimacy made life difficult in the great separation of a little room.

Why had the kissing stopped? Were her thoughts of another or was she mine? I needed her to speak to me like each plucked string from my bass guitar. To find the tongue that had hidden indoors. The echoing of the bass notes crept into my every nerve, especially when this lady wasn't such a lady. I bathed in the world between the waters of her cold, beautiful, dead eyes. If she had no room for me in her empty gaze, I could have been spared and never missed. A phrase searched for its form, for its weight, for its wings. Her silence spoke, ashamed of its joy. Lying by her side was not my proper place. I lay there like used equipment, batteries thrown aside waiting for the dust of passion to settle on her damp skin. In her heart there was another she dreamt about, beside her in his proper place. I was 'Mr Right Now' and I occupied her with a certain dull routine. Communication would hardly have mattered under the dark moon that clouds would not permit to shine.

I don't understand everything but the way it ended was no surprise. My girlfriend became pregnant and gave birth to a daughter, Vienna. But she didn't seem to have a mother's love for her child. She didn't want to become the guardian angel, the lifelong friend that a child needs. Perhaps the fact that Vienna was black raised the stakes too high for her. I worked torturous hours, almost silent on a freezing winter's day, treading a snow-filled landscape delivering leaflets; useless work just to make a penny. When I arrived home she sat on the couch, secure from what I wasn't sure. Perhaps from thoughts of that selfsame 'useless work', as she called it. She sat watching *Dallas* on a very loud television, smoking cigarettes, immune to a baby's cries, screams and moans. Vienna hadn't been changed all day, hadn't eaten and had cried so much that her voice had become hollow and faint. She held out her tiny arms to me as I took her in mine and held her world in my embrace. She needed the comfort of her father's love. I changed her and gave

THE JOURNEYMAN

her a bottle. Then indulged her with small treats while tucking her blanket around her.

One morning a note appeared on my pillow. It read, 'I'm not sure about us anymore. If we were in love surely I'd know it. Yesterday I felt one thing but today I feel something else. I'm very sorry.' She now sleeps under a glass piano. She gets up every morning and dances to her own sound around a huge deserted bonfire that flares, wind-driven, tended by the white man with money whom her parents approve of. There was no mention in the note of our daughter.

It was a cold autumn for weeks and more leaves had fallen. They would continue to fall until eventually they settled into a grave of brown dust.

I saw what frightened me most of all. I was 21 and hungry. No post had fallen through my letterbox. I was a single father without money or prospects, living day and night knowing money must be somewhere. I was, and still am, trying to manage without it. Everything had to connect on a shoestring. I was in arrears with the rent. White crumbling walls of damp surrounded my 11th-floor, concrete high-rise nightmare. Everything was clammy, not a dry patch to be found anywhere. I couldn't even light a match to ignite the cooker. The gas fire was always turned down as low as possible. Dirty nappies kept on coming, piled up against each other or shoved tightly into a bucket, not yet washed and destined to remain dirty. I had come from nowhere and I felt like I was going nowhere. Although it was cold outside, I set off down 11 flights of stairs with a pram through the stench of urine so strong it made my nose run and my eyes water. The lifts never worked. Vienna must have been used to the stale smell, as she was playing happily with a toy in her pram.

I was interested in music but I had nothing to sing about as I walked four miles to my mother's house, scaling long slopes behind the pram. I explained the situation to my mother. I explained the enormous odour I was living in and how close it was, the rotten floor, the bucket piled halfway up the walls with shitty nappies.

How Vienna scratched in her bed, though she seemed reassured in her burning piss-puddles. How I'd realised that I wouldn't be able to endure it another minute. I had pushed the pram along an uncertain road and felt sure that it was all beyond my control. Though I'd taken a long time to finally make up my mind, I took my daughter home to be raised by my mother and my sisters. Just as my mother had given her kids to her own mother and sisters. Hope seemed suspended above the rounded earth. I had seen it over and over, indifferently floating above my head. Every time I tried to reach it my hand would burn; the sky transmuted into a fire which fed on expectation. This was what I imagined knowledge, love and hope to be: something tantalising and painful, forever barred from me. This was my 21st birthday and no one had any idea.

Wasted minutes and hours were to follow. It couldn't have been worse. Nights of barbaric condescension as a nightclub bouncer staring out of doorways at passers-by. An inner voice kept on asking, 'Where are you going? What are you doing?' I would answer in the same tone of voice so no one could tell the difference between the inner and the outer voice. Innocently these conversations would engage the senses, only half meaning to, until there was no choice or sense. Alcohol crystallised the brains of those lost with no purpose. I heard nothing but the music through their nonsensical rambling as the DJ played another tune. The tension mounted, then lightened, then nothing except waiting. Occasionally some relaxed unpatronising stranger would emerge, releasing my heart and illuminating the nightmare hours I spent. The rest of the time was spent waiting or wrenching uneasy violent strangers out by their windpipes while they tried to breathe through elongated nostrils.

I practised my trumpet and bass guitar every day but they didn't feed me. Jazz wasn't going to make me rich. Then I opened a clothing business and sold the latest designer wear from Hong Kong, always careful to keep one step ahead of the people from the Department of Trading Standards. The business dried up after my supplier had to do bird for several years.

I had a brief affair with Mary Jane (marijuana). I craved her weight, her touch. Through the nights I hunted for a deal. I prowled silent streets. I hungered for her sleek length. I was like a dog on heat, desperate to smell her aroma. I paced around in those deserted hours, sniffing the dawn that interrupted my hunting. I remember opening my first bag as if I had opened life and heard death's faltering cry. I wrapped Mary in paper to prepare her for the burning. For me, smoking marijuana was an adventure that judged reason, set myself in mystery and bound the will in an iron chain as the smoke travelled down into receptive lungs. A night with Mary brought a throbbing to my temples and a burnt reality to the waking dawn. Once the novelty wore off I left her alone for boxing. Whatever I did I always remembered to keep my hands sharp in preparation for the coming seasons.

For a brief time I went to work as a bodyguard for various big-time moneymen, minding the money for those with no respect for poverty. All I wished was that they'd let some go, just let it fly with the wind. We are fragile monsters created by hard circumstance. Years have cultivated hate. Starved of love and tenderness, destruction becomes the preferred route. If I could, I would smash a right hand into the face of hunger, reach down into its belly and turn it inside out, smash it with infinite combinations, if only for a moment's peace.

I met a guy called Chris in a Manchester weightlifting gym and we became friends. Chris was just another boy from Manchester, from another council estate, from another centre of the world filled with hunger and pain. He was one of ten children. Each one had a different father and their mother downed her pills with whisky. The resentment Chris felt caused his mother more pain. He told me his probation officer had said to him, 'Time you took your life into your own hands and forgave your mother.' But a new man crept in silently through the door Chris had barred against the continuous agonies of numbers.

Chris wanted me to assist him in the grievous work of amassing wealth. He was doing illegal business and boasting of his skills. He was too proud to listen and refused to graduate from the heroic school of hard knocks that was the street. I wanted to save his life. I remember telling him that if he was to have the things he wanted out of life, there would be things he would have to give up. His answer is still very clear to me now: 'I'm not giving up anything. I'm a hustler. I'm gonna get paid. I'm gonna get mine.'

On the street all the arguments and all the posing are equally true. It's a fierce arena where disputing shadows settle their differences by visiting eternal sleep on each other, and it's nearly always about money. Chris had no way of escaping his hunger. He was streetwise but that knowledge was worth nothing against bullets that taught doubt and killed wisdom. These are the risks that boys run while they curse the game that represents their struggle for respect. They are prepared to be judged by the rules of the street's fiction. Chris' focus was on the many descriptions of a comfortable and wealthy life, without forgetting the life he knew.

One night, on an empty street surrounded by many houses, I found the dead body of Chris, pierced by bullets nobody had heard. He grew cold while people slept in warm beds only yards away. There were streaks of blood on their doorsteps. His arms were outstretched as if reaching out to his neighbours. His stare fixed blindly on the lost skies. I looked up and saw the moon disappear and reappear from behind black clouds, while lightning crumbled images. I raised my eyes to where the stars had set up camp, to a place where giant beings conspire to lie and observe the celestial bodies blink knowingly to each other. There seemed to be a faint smile on the boy's murdered mouth. Had he known it was the last time he would see such beauty? So young, a mother's child murdered. A father's son lost, lying dead in the street. He was a brother and a friend shot down in the street, wasted on a cowardly night. In the morning the bloodstained sidewalk brought terror to the neighbours, whose curtains had remained closed through the night, despite the sound of gunfire. What retaliation would there be for this man? In the safety of daylight the neighbours came out to see the hearse. But then, there's always sadness for a youth's coffin that passes through the streets where children hustle to survive. The murder remains unsolved.

The world was and is categorised by the superficial and external aspects of our existence. It was mastered and put into service. I saw a future where hungry children roam vast deserts in search of food. I saw mountains of food piled to the skies. I saw trees uprooted to make room for concrete and the cells that joined one man to another drained away in streams of contaminated blood. I saw man's vanity proclaim itself the purpose of the universe and was compelled by its hard reality to look beyond this physical world invented by lies. I could no longer defend myself from its illusions. I drifted through life like a cloud of smoke until, along rough streets, I found a fighter's path to a gymnasium full of hard men. So armed, I reached for the future with two creative hands.

7

CHORLTON STREET GYM

The gym was buried in the heart of Manchester's red-light district, Chorlton Street. Behind the gym independent working girls tossed off anonymous johns, all the time hiding the madness that fed their veins, the pain that poisoned their lives. I saw used condoms lying on the floor where they found their cash.

I wanted to box and I needed money. I approached Jack Trickett, a manager of fighters, and asked him, 'How does one go about becoming a paid fighter?'

He replied, 'What have you done? Have you ever been in a boxing ring and what do you do for a living?'

I told him, 'I have no interest in trophies. I've done some kick boxing and I play the trumpet.'

'Stick to music!' he answered

'Why don't you put me in the ring and see if I can fight?' I said.

They armed my spirit in leather, bound my hands, covered my head with a guard, found me a chewed-up gumshield and protection for my groin. I had followed my hands where they led. They were here to indulge themselves in their own pleasure. This was the first time I was to enter a boxing ring. A tiger never asks how to take its prey. It acts in the noon and eats in the evening.

John Jo Green was the Irish Light-heavyweight Champion. He was a tough southpaw (left hand forward), a brawler. Outside the ring he joked and clowned around carefree, but once the bell rang desire took flesh and compromise would leave his eyes, eyes that reflected a dream. His spirit was strong and knew its course. He rushed me with an unexpected barrage of punches. His intentions were bad. If no one made mistakes then we all would make them. Running into the unknown is always a bad move. Later our tortured souls would search for the meaning in dried blood.

Alone in a square ring I saw what needed to be done and adapted myself to the conditions. I began to look around me and listened, employing my entire body as other fighters did, relaxed but alert. That was the turning point in my life. How could I now go back to that other existence? I kept my eyes on the stars, reaching for them with both hands, unable to rest until I'd grasped my goal.

In my ferocious adolescence I read my fate in an old palm and I saw combat and great battles with faceless beings. I saw nights of bloodshed and ovations. I saw friends and bullies fall, the horizon collapse, sharpened fists that split skulls in two, a thirst for water and the wounds of detached lips. I saw giant lights beneath which men were cut down like tired trees by gloved axes, watched by stadiums of eyes. I saw arteries swelling in bruised necks, a man beaten to the ground and pride's whip goading him to get up again, only to be beaten down once more. I saw flesh devoured by pain and fatigue; battlegrounds where blackened eyes flogged themselves with impatience; a life that broke wills; a life that taught men the art of being masters of themselves. In those days glory reached out insistently, knocking on doors and inviting young men to sign on dotted lines.

A month after walking into the gym I was approached by Nat Baso, a promoter and MC. I had already signed with Jack Trickett but he asked me if I could fill in and fight Gypsy John Fury, another tough southpaw known on the cobbles as a 6 ft 3 in Irish bare-knuckle fighter. He also had a lot of experience inside the ring.

I expressed concern. 'I think it's too soon for a professional fight, Nat.'

Nat replied, 'If you're not going to fight, don't come back to this gym.'

It was a Friday night. The fight was going to be on Granada TV, in the *Fight Night* series, on the following Tuesday. They needed a heavyweight to save the show.

I agreed and asked Nat if he could lend me ten pounds until after the fight. 'Nat, it's raining cats and dogs outside. I need bus fare and I haven't had a decent meal in days.'

He pulled out a roll of 20-pound notes and held it up while he gave me a ten-minute lecture on budgeting that ended with 'Never a borrower nor lender be!'

I had to walk home approximately five miles in a thunderstorm knowing there would be no food in the cupboards when I got there.

Gypsy John Fury won a debatable decision in what was a very close fight and claimed a victory that came at the toss of a coin. I saw the whole experience as a crash course. I passed with a B grade. I wouldn't be beaten for the next few years. I liked Nat Baso because I always knew where I stood with him. Managers and promoters are the pimps, the fighters their whores. He died not too long ago. I was surprised. I thought he would live forever. I just couldn't imagine him giving away his last breath.

8

ANGELA

When I was young I had the strength of ten, or so I thought. Maybe I could have traded that boy's life for another but nothing is ever that easy. Now it seems that everywhere I go I travel through my own past, looking through windows of missed opportunities no longer open to me. But as a boy I had to believe I was invincible, to accept each choice as the right one. I lived off my will and determination. Nothing could stop me, not for a while, not until a cold woman passed through my life. She put her hand on my heart and left me frozen, a single parent with a daughter.

For the longest time I turned my back on love and love turned its back on me. It squatted in my house which, with its own set of keys, changed the locks and refused to let me in. I scratched my name on the front door with a pocket knife, beat my fists against the wood, threw rocks at the windows, but love never showed itself. Unable to leave it behind I forced my way in, only to find broken bits of furniture, cobwebs and debris. There was no one upstairs or down, in the attic or the cellar. I left that house of broken dreams, travelling through my mind, trying to find a place of tender memories. Tired and weary from my journey I stopped for a drink in an all too familiar place, and there, waiting at a table in the softest of lights, I saw my angel.

She sat at the opposite table to me in a crowded bar. She appeared shy and beautiful, with thick dark locks that reached halfway down her back and light brown eyes that ignored me. I fixed my eyes on her as she took tiny sips from a glass. I tried to imagine what she might be thinking. Unexpectedly she opened her legs and revealed her nakedness under the table. It wasn't an accidental flash. I pretended not to be looking but I was aroused by the outline of stiffened nipples beneath her blouse and the tight curls of her pubic hair, which was now visible. Her eyes searched my groin for signs of interest. Drawn to this woman who seemed to have been expecting me, wordlessly I sat at her table, our knees touching beneath it. I was aware of nothing beyond the way her hair curled softly down her neck, her sweet aroma and the slight pressure of her thighs against my own. She took my hand amidst the stares and whispers of the customers. We made our way to a bed where sheets were always fresh. I embraced her.

She stripped off and stretched out in front of me, naked, awaiting my touch. Her black body, burnt in the sun, stood naked, a beautiful statue holding on to its secrets. Secrets that had been betrayed by gin. Soft flesh perfectly formed, dimmed lights, each of us breathing deeply of the lust-filled air, while outside the wind played music amongst the trees. Silence spoke soft whispers, conversation was abandoned like a pause between two chords. With sparkling eyes, we bathed in each other's beauty, two naked beings made for each other. There was love in the meeting of eyes, in the meeting of radiant moons at first sight. That love suspended time, brought about an eternal living moment within which passions awoke to their realities. I stroked every inch of her with long supple fingers. Her heart pumped wildly and she found it difficult to control her breathing. There was a loud silence in which she looked at me and I was lost. Her finely sculptured lips came towards mine with all the passion I knew she possessed. She was made from my desires and grew out of my dreams. Her body was a magnet from which my world hung.

I don't believe that it was by chance that Angela, whom I had lost myself in, found me as if I were a wounded animal. To her I must have seemed from another age, carrying my fury into battle with ignorant hands. Her presence invaded and occupied me, rooting itself in me. It was the thing I desired most. Through my eyes she saw into my world, watched and studied me until I had no secrets. I never saw her coming, never heard a thing.

She didn't ask for much: just a little attention. I, on the other hand, I asked for everything without being demanding. I soon realised her strength as she accepted, gave her all, and covered my rage with tenderness. She fused with my being, dissolved herself into my bloodstream and devoured my will from the inside. Now she's entwined in my flesh forever with no escape, but she needn't be afraid because she became the meaning to this life I live. I had nothing to eat but dreams when she crept into my life and stayed. She was a beautiful black pearl with radiant eyes and well rounded thighs. But could she cook? She promised me I would not go hungry because she shared my dreams. Then she hugged me and told me that she loved me. She said she liked boxing and making love. But could she cook? She understood the relationship I had with my sport. I lived on the edge of experience, always between wakefulness and dangerous dreams, where life began. She understood all of it. But could she cook?

She gave me Cassius and then Clay, two perfect sons disguised as butterflies in all their glorious colours. They danced to their own shadows, throwing stinging combinations in the air. Their rhythms caressed my head and became one with my beating heart. I often lose myself in the dream of how they too will dance like a butterfly and sting like a bee. I hope they will know their calling. I always knew mine.

I understood the sacrifices that I had to make if I were to exist in an arena where being a nice guy doesn't count for anything. So I swam deeper than most into the pain, hoping someone would understand, that they would follow and rescue me from myself. But everyone I ever met rose for air except the woman who suckled my children. She pulled me from the water I sacrificed myself to and saved me from myself.

Her heart broke when she heard the tale of a life at the bottom of the world. She listened to the trumpet I played for a penny in a hat. But how long could she save me from the type of hunger I had, the type that could last a lifetime? She understood my hopes and dreams. She saw the potential I had to knock out heavyweights. In September 1991, I became the Central-area Heavyweight Champion, knocking out Carl Gaffney in eight rounds in Stockport. I remained undefeated. She saw his blood run like an oil slick and, like always, waited for my return from hell anticipating my gentle and soft touch. I would walk through the door and she would hit me in the mouth with a kiss, long and passionate. A fighter who was a lover and her love was total. Before children we'd spend days locked into the dazzle of desire, swept away in whirlwinds of passion, with no wish for calm.

I was happy to be at home with Angela and the children but I longed for the ringing of a bell. I would begin listening to the inner voice no man can ignore. The fight never leaves the blood. Silent hands, black nights, a slave to circumstance. Long evenings of raging blood that would surge through enlarged veins. Knuckles that obstructed breathing and tested the spirit. Finally, the blow that would be as silent as a sword slicing through the air. Advice to young warriors: if you drop a man, stand over him just in case he tries to get up so you can knock him down again. Why let him off? So he can get up and hurt you? There's no room in the ring for mercy. The lessons you give him will be learnt, have no fear. After looking back at the tape, seeing himself out cold and hearing his lady crying, he'll never make the same mistake again, I promise you! After every round the devil dies and hope is born anew. Don't waste time looking behind you, living is here and now.

Angela wanted to be a singer who could capture the moment with a phrase and set it to air. A singer who could take a song and fill the vast dimensions between man and the world around him, who could create innocent dreams with a verse, although her innocence was lost in an age of fulfilment. A singer who can force an audience to sing in joy with a melody, who could inspire lovers with blue notes, and stretch out without fear. All she had to do was overcome the hindrance of nerves. Then she could appear before an audience who waited for the singer Angela could truly be. She was made from the vocal cords of all men. She was the scale that balances melody and harmony, the sound that would soothe the heads of men, an everlasting sound that would grow from the hearts and dreams of the living. A great voice that every night closes its eyes to listen to itself, while its body rises through streams of sound to be borne into the air. Angela liked to listen to Billie Holiday, a singer who was possessed by music. That great voice had hung on to herself with her nails and teeth, fighting the need for drugs that would eventually destroy her. Her heartache was like the mist first thing in the morning. Her pain carved vinyl tracks. When the lights dimmed, Angela could submerge into such depths.

Angela had just finished her first gig in a hotel after-dinner dance. 'Tonight you were fantastic,' I told her. I let my tired body sink into the mattress. 'You sang with dry lips and my head was burning. I wanted to sing with you and express the sensation of the joy you gave me. I watched you chart your way through unknown melodies. Now I am trying to sing them because they are still present in my head, vibrating through my brain. Tonight will glow in my memory when I remember it like this in all its wonderful sound. There will be no pain remembering it. I will remember you first, the way your smile sweetened the moment, the way you held the microphone, and each kiss we shared. Come to bed and share what's left of the night before it moves to day. Life moves on day by day. It leaves nothing behind and never comes back. Lie by my side. Let us raise our voices in passion. Let us not be in a hurry to get up. Let us ignite one more sparkling kiss that will last us until another night like this.'

Later I heard the silence disturb itself in the black night so I got up and walked across the bedroom until I came to a stop. With half-closed eyes I saw through glass another body. I think it was the one I wanted. I say 'think' because I wasn't sure to what extent I was dreaming. He stared straight at me with fixed eyes like he wanted to occupy me and fuse his flesh with mine. I stared back. We stood face to face for quite some time waiting to be introduced, neither wanting to commit himself or do anything about the long silent pause. Then I realised that I was standing in front of my bedroom mirror and he was me. I extended my hand to offer friendship and we both began to laugh. Then I went back to a dream where I saw angels without eyes. They stood guard over me between night and day, a time when the soul shakes in battle with self-doubt.

There was a time before the fight was born in me. Before the birth of hope, when doubt prevailed. I stood alone on the edge of decisions unable to indulge in dreams. It was a time when I almost drowned in the uncertainty of my mother's milk. When the sun set, I doubted that it would rise again. When I was hungry, I questioned whether I would eat again. When I was in love, I was unsure it would last. Now I slept in a bed of dreams side by side with the woman I fell in love with. That morning I woke with an inextinguishable fire and took on the day.

The parental bonds which are natural to both of us can't be found in everyone. Angela's original parents are an example. At four months old Angela's foster parents were sad to see her go but felt safe in the knowledge that, being good people, Ian and Norah were adopting her and would provide a loving home that would allow her to be steady on her feet. They took a black child from a foster home into their white family. They already had one son of their own but were unable to have a second. Later Angela was to get a younger brother, as so often happens, when her parents had relaxed.

Throughout her childhood Angela lived in a white neighbourhood. Some encounters with white kids in her area created a sore inside her that burns when I touch it. Some adults were no different. Black children learn how to defend themselves against their antagonists. But the attention they have to pay to others is a distraction, and can cost valuable time and resources. Angela spent her childhood explaining to friends, peers and neighbours why her parents were white. Hearsay came muffled, distorted, diminished through the grapevine to her safe place.

The system of adoption invites certain dissatisfaction, especially from the viewpoint of a black person. Could I, as a black man with a black family, adopt a white child? My father-in-law, Ian, strongly agrees that prejudice would make it most unlikely that a black family could do so. He tells me that when he and Norah applied to adopt a baby with no other qualification than that it should be a girl it was made clear to them that if they didn't specify a white child they would be offered a mixed-race baby. Ian said, 'It seems that Whites want White, Blacks want Black, Chinese want Chinese, Asians want Asian and so on. So, prejudice aside, babies are placed with families where they are most likely to blend with the background.'

Mixed-race children are the exception. Luckily for Angela, Norah and Ian told me they can't distinguish white from black. Ian even questions why little girls with Jamaican fathers and white Mancunian mothers are regarded as black when they are clearly just as much white. In spite of this, although it was unvoiced, Norah felt, perhaps instinctively, that Angela would be safer with a non-white partner and was delighted when she started looking for 'black' boyfriends. If it is possible for a black child in a black home to go mad with self-disgust, then the moon be thanked for what her parents achieved.

This is a white world and they have the power to choose. Mixed-race babies aren't always placed with families where they are most likely to blend with the background. To most people a person of Jamaican and British origin isn't clearly as much white as they are black. Do we consider Bob Marley as much white as he is black?

Angela grew up fantasising about celebrity parents but her fairy-tale dream of being contacted by famous black singers soon disappeared from view when she thought about leaving or being without her adoptive parents. On her 18th birthday her parents told her that her birth certificate and papers were available to her. They told her that they understood the need to know who she was. As distant a memory as it is, she had other parents, other than the ones that nurtured her throughout her life. Thoughts of a perfect meeting and acceptance have long left her mind, though it still needs an image to melt the memory of a blind longing into a dream.

I'd met Angela on a Friday and on the Monday she appeared with a suitcase. 'I take it you're moving in?' I said.

'I certainly am,' came the reply.

We've been together ever since. She was introduced to my brother Lance, who never spoke to her, and to my sisters, whose views on men at the time, especially towards me and my house habits, could have sent her packing back to her parents. However, she stood her ground with her already-developed plan of how to create a man that couldn't be without her. It must have been a good scheme because it worked. We were married on 5 June 1992 and I've never looked back.

At that time, Angela's daily routine was fairly domesticated. She would start the day by digging me in the ribs, saying, 'Come on, wake up. Wake up, you're dreaming. It's time to go running.'

'Who's been dreaming? I've been running already.'

'I'm going to make some breakfast, are you having any?'

Usually when I tried to get up the bed got bigger and I couldn't find my way off it.

Angela also rose early without excitement and prepared breakfast for our children. They had toast, cereal, or whatever she could find in the cupboards. All the while her mind was on the work ahead: the hard path through mountains of clothes. Another few days and the children would be off school for a couple of weeks, maybe a chance for a lie-in. Well, she could give it some thought. She went on preparing lunch-boxes and ironing school uniforms, after which she crammed the children into the car and took them to school.

Sometimes when she came home, she hesitated for a moment, then made a decision. Something entirely out of character: the work could wait. She had time for herself and the whole day open to her. But then she decided she would deal with first things first: the washing up; shopping; preparing the meals for the evening; tidying up; polishing; hoovering; washing clothes and cleaning the bathroom and bedrooms. So she got cracking.

She lived in the wash basket she carried to the washing machine everyday, and when I was home something sparkled in my eyes when I saw her bending over to put the washing into the machine, the clothes piled at her feet. When I look at Angela from behind I can't tell you how beautiful her body is with its voluptuous curves. I know that the work she does is important but when my gaze is fixed on her rear . . . Anyway, she already knows my transparent mind, its perversions and the single thought that runs through my head.

She worked hard all day. Love and hate came into it. Would anyone show their appreciation? Would her anger rise if they didn't? She made some phone calls. Then made some more which in turn created the need to make some more. By evening she was worn out and stopped to make notes on phone calls she would have to make in the morning if she wanted to stay on top of things. When she looked up it was dark outside but finally everything was done, clean and tidy. Clothes were in drawers, no doubt waiting the arrival of muddy hands. She had done everything she could think of, everything she felt she had to do. It was what her sense of duty told her must be done, without disappointing anyone. At that moment sitting in her tidy house she was nagged by the memory of the time she had wanted but never got: time for herself.

She often walks past me in the bedroom wearing nothing, her locks thrown over her shoulders as though spring had just arrived in the middle of winter. She passes me with confidence and pretends not to notice lustful eyes following her across the room as I lie in bed. I love her scent as she creeps into bed at night before I dream.

I know for sure that anything that smells that good and feels so soft and warm must be fantastic. Then my body, like any properly tuned motor, turns on over her sensitive skin, felt through a labyrinth of nerve endings.

Angela came across confident but on the inside she was insecure. She was a good person without malice; a warm dream about to be dreamt. There was a time when she tried to explain her lack of confidence but soon realised it was a mistake because nobody believed her. She was desperate to find something that could give her the confidence she needed to achieve a purpose in life.

I encouraged her to go back to school and take the course in acting she'd always been dreaming about. Maybe she could learn to cover up the fact that she was a nervous person. She had my full support and I was able to stay at home with the children. She learnt fast and developed the skill of making believe she was someone else. She found the profession to which she was destined. She was now an actress who on stage played a character to an audience that in turn accepted her as the stage persona.

Nightly she sees herself reflected in a thousand mysterious eyes. She already knows by heart a hundred different parts and needs only a spark to move from one to another through a shifting mind. The enthusiastic approval by knowledgeable critics of her timing, rhythm and presence is what she now craves. All she needs is the right phrase to dispel sleep from the weakest mind, rather than boring it with carelessly chosen words plucked from the heads of uninspired writers. Soon a swarm of feet will pass through an already worn out auditorium. Soon doubt will be silenced as she presses her reluctant passion into performance. All dreams that make for happiness are good dreams. I never doubt the soul's sincerity.

While Angela was learning about acting, my time spent with my children led to the discovery of a new creative urge within me. I regained my imagination, seeing red the way others see it. Their eyes were free from the association of pain with the colour of blood. I began watching people as they spoke about life and measured their enthusiasm. I noticed that no one ever praised the setting sun or spoke of beauty, though women consider it for hours in mirrors. There seemed to be so many unspoken feelings and inexpressible thoughts in people. My reawakened enthusiasm led me to poetry, which could explain so much: the glory of the night; the stars; the moon; the soft breeze; the shadows and the light. It forced me to pick up a pen and weigh the value of words. Their illusions and their ability to lift us up in our darkest moments make sense of the madness around us. Even though the past was already scripted, now I could make my pen write its own story. I peered through my skull's black window wondering what could credibly help me to express the silent thoughts and words that came flooding into my vision. Thoughts pierced like an arrow, spoken through the pen's strangled throat. All I attempted to do was write, aware that my boyhood, bereft of the ability to do the same, had vanished without so much as an echo.

My younger self hadn't been the only one to suffer this fate. As a child I had seen men with haunting voices turn into ghosts, because people no longer listened to them. I suppose this is what happens when the desire to speak becomes so subversive that we only communicate through whispers. I hope my pen achieves something different; that my words grab your mind by the scruff of its neck, strangle ignorance and spread like a virus by word of mouth. I've written in a tongue I hope will cross blue seamless skies and cover continents.

THE JOURNEYMAN

9

CHAMPS CAMP

I started training at Moss Side Champs Camp in 1988. Now I had a new routine to the mornings. Sometimes they'd start with Angela tearing my T-shirt and pants off me, but after my run and breakfast they'd always move on to packing my gym bag: shorts; boxing boots; gum shield; groin guard; towel; deodorant; bandages; T-shirt; underpants; socks; bag gloves; sparring gloves; head guard and Vaseline; tape for my hands; face cream; courage; self-belief and confidence. I put in a good jab, good footwork which gave me plenty of mobility, a pair of fast hands with a variety of punches, eye contact, concentration and, most importantly, a little luck. Then I set off towards Moss Side.

When the passions of blind people who see well enough are spent the stars make no comment. My aim was to make enough money to eat, to build a nest, even on the nights when the battle ended in dark defeat. I was a lean and well-trained athlete. My feet gripped the canvas and the blind crowded in to see me fight. There was a naked truth about a naïve mind born into naïve days. I smiled with innocence. I trained under Phil Martin, an ex-fighter who had contested the British Light-heavyweight title in the 1970s and lost over fifteen rounds. He was a hard man who fought without comment but felt the need to rage against the error of being born poor, as do most fighters. Though that isolated him from other trainers, managers and promoters, he was merciless in pursuit of his vision. He took a derelict building, long abandoned and gutted by fire in the 1981 Moss Side riots. It was covered in graffiti, as were the concrete jungles of the high rise flats that darkened the skyline. Moss Side had a fearsome reputation and unemployment ran high, though there are even worse areas in Manchester. Phil built a stable of formidable fighters. It was something he did with a government grant.

The ring had all the answers. It showed him its hidden prizes and he saw everything. Once his own career was over he bound and unbound brilliant hands with tape. He prepared young boys for the empty hours that served their needs and his. Phil taught me how to be a journeyman in the best possible sense. He would say, 'If you can't go away from home at anytime and fight to win in another man's back yard you might as well forget it!'

That's the policy I've followed throughout my career. You might get robbed now and then but you must be able to handle yourself away from home. You can either fight or you can't. It's that simple.

The gym always looks the same when you enter. The steam rises from hot bodies. Lactic acid was calculated in habit-forming grafting routines. Tired men stretched like tired cats. Time slowed to a march: sit-ups; warm down; counting gym fees. I would go for a shower, and remember the last moments of a dream: my arms raised in victory, and returning home to the waiting arms of the most beautiful woman I knew in waking life – as apart from the fantasies of erotic sleep.

A cassette of James Brown played over and over in the place where warriors prepared for battle. Their thoughts were of their children laughing happily in the lives their fathers had made for them. Even the men who the fight had crushed brought a roar of pride into the gym. A wind blew through the open windows and cooled sweating foreheads. The memories of nights spent lying in pools of blood were washed away when the water from the shower splashed onto our faces, revitalising strong bodies that might otherwise go to waste on the mean streets of the outside world. I often stayed awhile to watch other fighters training. Men like Ensley Bingham, a former Light-middleweight Champion. Maurice Core, a former Light-heavyweight Champion. Carl Thompson, a former Cruiserweight Champion. Paul Burke, a former Lightweight Champion. Tony Ekubia, a former Light-welterweight Champion. Frank Grant, a former Middleweight Champion. Joey Jacobs, a former Super-featherweight Champion.

Phil became paranoid about those who hadn't signed contracts with him, to the point of leaving a tape recorder in the changing-rooms. One day after training I opened my front door to his anger, insults and accusations: apparently I was trying to turn fighters against him. He held up a small tape recorder to prove his argument and pressed play. I was horrified to recognise the voices of fighters who had worked out that afternoon. He had recorded all that we had said, eyes blinded and breathless. On hearing my voice I recalled my statement in the original conversation with another fighter, Ozzie Maddix. He owed Phil money and in front of the whole gym, while we cooled down from the exercises, Phil told him to keep the money. Later in the changing-room Maddix asked me what I thought. I told him that he should pay back the money because there would be too many strings attached to it and that before he knew it he'd be signing contracts. I repeated it to Phil. That was my opinion and I hoped he would take the trouble to evaluate the seriousness of what he'd done. He retreated in confusion but after that there was an atmosphere in the gym. The air became heavy, like a leaden weight.

A pennywise upbringing must have taken Phil's days and moulded them into a hard outlook without human compassion. While he had one arm around my shoulders congratulating me the other was in my pockets helping himself to the money he felt he deserved. When I confronted him he told me, 'I'm the best trainer in the country. I'm worth the money and if you don't like it you know where the door is!' I disagreed and cleared out my locker.

As I left Champs Camp I experienced an odd kind of daydream. The vanishing light escaped unchallenged, its memory faded to an unheard darkness that reflected in my eyes and purified my vision. As I walked through the silent gym I saw someone who looked like me, his ribcage open, guts all over the gym floor. He must have been lying there for a long time while creatures searched for gold, jewellery, whatever prospectors look for in a man's pocket after he is dead. Then came more scavengers to claim a share of whatever was left on his decomposed corpse. As I looked on I realised it wasn't just money they wanted, it was his soul.

It takes at least two to make a fight. The mind, on the other hand, fights with itself. If you run away breathlessly you only begin another fight, for better or worse, until you find another direction. Only the fight was sure. Who could have told me what was about to come? Outside of the moment of the fight, it was too easy for the mind to react to everything else with emotions. Emotions that hold us, play with us and discard us, fight as we may.

The vision in the gym gave rise to a lot of thought about my life. A broken heart cast shadows where I stood. I had trusted Phil. A hard life had embedded itself in my vulnerable flesh and its sharpened hands now cut off my breathing with well-timed blows. Blows which seemed to unmask my fighting career for what it was. In packed arenas spectators recline comfortably on expensive chairs while witnessing victories and despairing defeats. But victories are short-lived and never really exist while promoters, trainers and managers cast their shadows, flying high like vultures over the bodies of both the fallen and victorious equally. Our bleeding hearts are racked with questioning doubt and our minds seared with the pain of our bloody economic realities. Yet we are filled with the desire to win and to curse the ugly reminders that tell us that life comes down to ourselves. For a time I was motionless. The exposure to a future was denied. The lies behind warm smiles conspired with greedy eyes. My stock had crashed but eager hands still groped in my pocket for what change they could find. Primitive organs spilled their seeds as they fucked me over.

I had risen from a guttered past to the stillness of a dead end. Not even in combat had I felt a battle's bitter kiss so sour. I would have felt better if I had not been born and even better not to have been born twice. Especially not being reborn in the gym on Chorlton Street where my dream had caught fire. I sank with millions of others into the hell of self-pity. What was real? Which eye saw and exactly how many were there? Which limb moved first? Was anything independent in our arrangement of legs and arms, eyes and atoms? To the mind aren't they all just mirrored reflections of themselves? And why couldn't the person standing in front of the mirror be in doubt? What if we were just reflected errors? My reflected certainty was broken and the question was: could I readjust to a new design of the present?

Whilst I was at Champs Camp Angela spoke to me about having a baby girl. Although she had accepted my daughter Vienna as her own, and given me two boys, the empty crib made an enormous shadow on the bedroom wall. We decided to have another go. I controlled my passion, waiting for the most appropriate time. When it happened, I embraced the pulsating strength of that new moment, gradually increasing in rhythm until my seed took root. We were happy and eager to see what flower or fruit would grow from this, knowing that each seed grows into a face.

We both imagined what the new child would be like, but our vision of her face seemed too real to be a dream. This beautiful woman held in her womb the seed of all my passion and would soon be giving birth to more joy created in her image. Our souls grew closer every day. I got to know Angela so much better through our dream of a new child. She had so much energy. Pregnancy was meant for a woman of her nature. She absolutely revelled in the glow of it all.

But come the birth, blood seemed to bring a moment's wonder which dissolved into the walls of Angela's womb. Would the baby become nothing more than an inaccessible thought after her dream ended? The night before our daughter's birth, I'm sure the finger of God invented a star that knew who she was, where she'd been, and what she hoped for. It watched over a million unborn bodies plus the one to which she belonged for nine months and imagined each breath that would interrupt her silent lungs for a brief moment. Then the star patiently waited for the last breath that came too easily. I dreamt of things we could have done: words she never spoke; the life she never lived; the hopes she never shared; the dreams she never fulfilled. Premature baby girl, the stillborn, still, unborn. The devil mocked and laughed at our dissatisfaction in him, but the baby was still wanted and needed. The life that once roamed inside her, shaped by the womb that held it, was silent by Nature's will. Despite Angela's grief, her need to love was stronger than any demon or god.

One morning shortly after, I got up at 6 a.m. It was still dark. One foot of the sun steadied itself on my window sill. A milk float had just passed my door. It was very cold and I wanted and needed a cup of hot coffee, knowing that in the winter the sun would not warm me. I stood up, stretched, walked to the window and looked out onto the street. A man stepped out of a shadowed doorway. He stood for a minute alone, looking around. What was he waiting for? A miracle? But I knew he waited for me. He was looking up at my window. We had arranged to run when the darkened sky died. Rest should have been enough for aching eyes that dare to dream. Even if you wake up to the long road of another day. Its sweat and strain are living evidence of the path's loneliness and its everlasting joy.

I went down to follow the road's adventure because it was there. The morning brings more clarity than the night. I'm able to see the bitter irony of fate and the vanity of all things human. I know a fighter's pride in the ring away from life's monotonous drag. God gave me talent, though I'm not worthy of his giving. He must have had some faith in me. As we ran my friend asked why I fought. How does one answer that question? I started by explaining we all die, so how do we live? The truth is I have no idea but I keep going. Even though I look after this body it is still dying. Nothing I can do about that.

Perhaps the answer is very simple. Angela and I are both fighters. We carry on because what will be, will be. When it rains a river swells. When there's a thunderstorm a child is afraid. I fight, not intending to upset your faint hearts, but in spite of the fact. Your life isn't my life. I've dreamt of living apart from this poverty in another body that refuses to take the crumbs from your table. I fight for my own reasons with or without your approval. Every privilege, however obscure, is a miracle we take for granted. My friend and I ran home with a dark breeze against our faces into the comfortable lives that freed our minds from the ordeal of weariness.

For all that I have, I know there will come a time when it simply isn't enough. I can remember walking into the gym one morning to find it buzzing in amazement with talk of a fight the night before. We were all gossiping, while fists slammed into hanging bags, about a fighter we trained with every day. Some said he was finished or that maybe the sport was finished with him. I'd seen him on television. He didn't want to show his bruises. He was hiding a pair of blackened eyes behind dark glasses. He just looked as if he wanted to escape from the yellow contaminated air he was now breathing, to take a holiday away from himself. I felt they should have let that courageous man just be brave; they shouldn't have let the false claim of him being fearless go waltzing across a dance floor in its own blood before they knew what it meant. The newspaper headlines read 'A Questionable Heart': they wanted a tender piece of meat and they ate well but remained hungry. People find it difficult to find sympathy for an absence of courage in someone. It's just too ugly. Some said he deserved a second chance to save face. I say you should know when to face reality. How can you disapprove of your true nature? I read his story and saw him become a victim of brave corner men. I saw the stool in his corner and yet they tried to send him back out for more of the same. His own corner caused his shame and forced him to quit on his stool. After the disgrace of refusing to fight on he tried to slide out of the back door without realising that his actions would be sent out across the airwaves to be frozen on a television screen for the whole world to see. He never came back to the gym, but when I heard that he was making a comeback I decided to write him an anonymous letter and signed it 'A Fan'. Of course, he knew my handwriting. I don't remember the exact words of the letter I wrote but it went something along the lines of:

> Once upon a time you practised moves in the mirror, danced and threw endless numbers of combinations that came like the fluttering wind. You'd break into a sweat, take off your T-shirt and imagine you were Sugar Ray. You trained hard in those days, pushed to the limits of a trainer's obsession. However, the last time you stared at yourself in the mirror did you see how your belly danced with a mind of its own? I know you probably went on your toes with a bounce, hands against your chin, legs spread wide, fists clenched tight and threw a hook or two that felt great. Those are the hooks that reel you in on the bitter round of comebacks, just one more fight. I know how it happens. I understand the need for another adrenaline fix. I see the signs, the room converted into a gym, the new equipment. Your fans can't help you find your youth, and your vanity will be useless in a game of pain. There was a time when you could slide in and out of anyone's hands but today you'd be caught under heavy fists, too heavy for you to rise again. Your reputation will burn on the tongues of fire. Stay a hero in our memories. Once upon a time you were incredible and always will be to me.

It wasn't long after that I fought someone just like my friend, at the G-Mex Centre in Manchester, in front of 7,500 spectators. He was an old pro ignoring his years, an American named Rocky Sekorski, the Minnesota Heavyweight Champion. He had never been knocked out and had taken part in many professional fights against the best heavyweights in the world. Men like George Foreman and Larry Holmes. Before the bell rang to begin our show I looked into his eyes. They were blinded by desire. He avoided looking back. But how could he imagine what he hadn't yet experienced? The blood ran down his face from a gash where knuckles had torn his flesh. There was nothing in the corner man's kit that could stop the bleeding. That night I found the old pro stiff, slow and easy to hit. He could do nothing except watch as I attacked his wounds and ripped apart his bloody face. Then he looked at me with a desire I could not break and cursed my mother. If he closed his eyes for a second he could have been lost in a dream on the canvas. He was the epitome of a journeyman. He fought for his life, his living. He was the hero who always rose from the floor. He was willing to fight anyone, anywhere, with only a moment's notice. This journeyman stalled for more time and tried to find his heart but my fists made it clear he was finished. He was done for and he knew it. No one could help him. We all witnessed his downfall and saw him reduced to a mouse trapped within a cat's paws. I looked to the referee to save him and take it out of the doctor's hands before his humiliation went any further. No one did a thing, not until his corner reached for the towel and tossed it over the ropes.

I studied his battered and embarrassed face and I thought all his life he wanted to be a fighter, a champion. So how could the towel save him from his dream? His eyes were clear but he knew that the time had finally arrived, to say goodbye to the life he was living. He had looked at me with hungry eyes. His hands were still sharp. He had looked at the referee who stood expecting the worst. Then he collapsed and became lost in a dreamy vision of a lost galaxy for at least fifteen minutes. He felt the touch of concerned hands on his shoulder. A voice asked 'What's your name?' Followed by another 'How many fingers do you see?'

Then an out-of-focus hand slowly became clear, as did the realisation of his mortality. From that day he never fought again. A story went around about how he'd die slowly from the lack of soul and that eventually his heart would have an attack of boredom. The problem was and still is that you can't take the fight out of a fighter without first taking his soul. That is, unless a man can say of his life or of any moment of his life that there is nothing more to be desired.

In the morning I climbed the stairs to the gym and reached for my boxing gloves hung above a picture from my last fight. I took them down, put them on and relived the fight when I got up on the count of eight only to be backed onto the ropes. I remember spraying the first row of screaming faces with my blood, and the woman who stood up and shouted, 'Knock him out!'

The next spray splashed across her dress. I climbed out of the ring and she came behind me and hit me in my back. 'Look what you've done to my dress!'

I gave her the number to my hotel room and she came, still wearing her bloodstained dress and said, 'Where's the money?'

Her name was Angela but she preferred Angie. I asked her to peel the tape from my hands. Then she started to lick and kiss my wounds. She mounted me and said, 'Show me what you can do!' I had to push her off to stop the flow of blood from my eye. She seemed aroused by a bloody nose, broken hands, battered body, blackened and bleeding eyes. It all seemed a good reason for me to plunge inside her.

The most talented of all who trained in Moss Side was Ensley Bingham. His left hook was a thing of beauty. I watched it blow swiftly over our heads, as men of flesh wore themselves down to breathing shadows, until the last light was out. I witnessed the battle harden the physical errands for us, how we wandered through crowds of shadows focusing on the pain ahead. Posing officials stood deep, already in their own shadows, in a place where business is conducted by a million screaming hands. In the middle of this sea, on a clouded canvas, the searchlights raised gloved hands to applause, pressing them upwards against time, withholding seconds and the inevitable pain. Men laboured proud against time. Half-naked in only shorts and boots they created concerts, composing with hands. Bingham's left hook blew swiftly over our heads, rehearsing its delivery before crashing down on a man's chin, sending him back to his own shadow. A dark certainty. Bingo, lights out! They stood among the broken shades of large punch bags, staring at the clock. Strange warriors, men with familiar aching muscles, dripping with sweat, wanting time to speed its pulse. Fighting is waiting and building the patience to endure calm necessity. They had fought through long rounds with torn flesh in naked rings, but there they stood, held by the minute, gasping for air without urgency, quietly forgotten.

10

SHANNON'S GYM

After leaving Champs Camp I drifted from gym to gym but mainly I used The Fox. It used to house many of the best amateur and professional fighters from the Manchester area. I had lost my faith in trainers so on fight nights I used corner men like Brian Hughes or Deni Mancini, but mostly I used Ray Farrell, a trainer employed by my manager, Jack Trickett. I continued training by myself until I met Bob Shannon around 1995.

Bob was a former amateur boxer but he vacated the violent arena for a standard life, a nine to five, a wife and kids. He grew tired of the travel beyond action. It was too far so he came back to training and preparing young fighters, something he'd grown up watching his father do. Bob is a youthful trainer with a lot of energy and the hope of training a champion. But first he has to stand in line and queue for his title winner. His first contender was Wayne Rigby, a lightweight who had come up against Michael Ayres in two great fights and lost both times. I've always liked Ayres. He is a true warrior with one of the biggest hearts in boxing. Bob's second contender was Mike Holden, a heavyweight I'd taken apart like a statue made of Lego bricks. He'd lost the taste for the ring and wanted out. So what purpose had Bob now? I suppose he sensed the chance to create something out of the situation, out of his life. Bob has a type of blind longing that melts the memories of heroes into dreams. Luckily the dream is lighter than a feather on a flying bird. He follows in his father's footsteps, hoping he inherited something tangible from a good trainer.

Following my fight against Danny Williams, we were putting the finishing touches to our training along with a friend whose name, I'm ashamed to say, I don't even remember. He was in the ring with his sparring partner. Between rounds someone at ringside remarked how his legs had lost their spring. He had no bounce and looked unstable on his feet. His punches had no zip. He just didn't look so hot. 'Are you okay?' we asked. 'Have you had your medical yet?'

This isn't an easy way to make a living. The next day my nameless friend went for his annual brain scan. They found a tumour the size of an orange, took his arm and gave him a month, no longer. When I saw him a week later he looked the same but different, maybe a few pounds heavier. I put my arms around him and gave him a hug. I was afraid he might fall to pieces. We talked for a while about boxing, but it was hard to pay attention to what he was saying. All I could think about was how does it feel to know that next month you'll be dead? Something came into his eyes when he talked about fighting and in those moments I knew he felt fine. That's all he wanted to talk about, nothing else. He wanted to know when I was going to fight and who, about training and the gym, but didn't have time to wait for answers and began to talk some more. Then he finally said it, 'I'm going to die!' We touched fists and hugged once more. Then he turned and went.

What I remember most about him was his energy and his will to win. He kept fighting until he reached the final bell even though he was well beaten. I know that energy of his is still out there somewhere. On its toes shadow boxing night and day, refusing to rest until he reaches that winning round where only he'll know when enough is enough. Then he'll gracefully retire to some infinite corner of time and space. A poor young warrior in search of dignity and respect, all the while retaining his faith – a gut feeling, a belief strictly human – dependable in times of confusion and pain. This life takes the ones we love for its own twisted reasons. It's just an ordinary thing, this energy generated by our lives. It seems immobile, a transference of pure self that rolls around from person to person in an external galaxy. That's my gut feeling.

My own dark shadow stands alone in the centre of a universe surrounded by four ropes waiting for the certainty of death; or, as I see it, a transference of my energy. The horizon will be wiped away with a left hook. A toothless mouth will open its black hole and swallow me. It will digest and fuse me into its dark walls until I can no longer distinguish my conscious mind from the unconscious mind offered to me by the prearranged darkness. Its thoughts already fixed, this world knows my fate.

Bob convinced me to try and get myself in shape. I'd not fought for a while. I took to the road and was disappearing under a rapid pulse. The road appeared to have been abandoned. Whatever meaning the morning had also appeared to have been abandoned. The road seemed to be dissolving under a mist in all directions. Somehow the mist incorporated my pulse. Gleaming with wetness I ran through an indefinite, unshaped dawn with a vacant, half-lit mind. My heart was beating for the sake of a brave drum. It was the hour when unfit lungs are drained of oxygen. I continued along the road punctuated by the occasional driverless vehicle. Odd trees dropped into the foreground like lost pimples on a teenager. Miles of greyish red-brick houses stood, admirable structures made stone by stone, but they had little to say for themselves. A small bus with few passengers moved smoothly along the road in tune with my pace. It passed close by and the passengers watched me disappear behind it in the mist. The birds began singing but the music didn't quite come through. It came in snatches, dim and keen, muted, and yet there was no breeze. I think the trees must have intervened, catching the music in their leaves like gold dust.

The moon was still visible. She looked out a million miles with pride in herself, far away beyond sleep. She is after all a daytime sleeper, a mutation from an insomniac's dream of an inverted world where left is always right, where the shadow I followed home was really my body. She had stayed awake all night. I also would be going back to bed while the rest of the world got up for work. I ran in a tracksuit and trainers I had bought from the best sport shops. Some say I'm mad and that today's athletes run on treadmills in warm central heated buildings: the intelligent way to train. But I prefer the beautiful outdoors with no machines. That morning I ran along a road that disappeared into a dusty, grey mist. All I could see was the face of my next opponent, Herbie Hide, whose eyes stared fixed on mine, doubting me. I could hear screaming from the other side of the mist and the cries from the blazing throats that always ask for blood. The mist is what it is. It whispers the names of fighters who existed in time and moved through this world, honouring contracts, trying to gain respect and feed families. I ran against the clock, trying to make eight miles inside the hour. Flying through the mist the hour felt wrong, but there was no time to wake from this dream about early morning roadwork.

Obsessions are at the root of all our lives, nothing we can do about that. Give me some credit – I'm somebody's father and it was early. Imagine yourself with young mouths to feed and your fists your only skill. Maybe if I'm lucky I'll be born again into another place. I was nearly home despite the fatigue that invaded my body.

The umbilical cord which sustained me, the career as a fighter, was fed to me until I no longer recognised myself, a cord I jumped through everyday, endlessly spinning round, never satisfied. The knots of that cord became so tight they pulled me down, with enough force to immobilise me. I tried denying anything which taught me I was a slave, which told me my will belonged to a way of life. I denied the breast that forced its milk into me. Nature threatened me with its fist. Shining bright, the sun set against me and began to burn, furious with my disbelief. I fought hard and the sun retreated back to its place but sent savage birds to watch over my alert and dissatisfied mind.

In vain I tried to free myself from the shadows that always seemed to be following me. Even though I knew in reality that the shadows belonged to me and I was wasting time escaping, escaping only to be followed again. I am no more free to choose than when I began this life but I refuse to fall in my own pointlessness and be beaten by this body that chooses to fight without choice. Maybe if I decided to stop fighting I would come into life and be born again into another body whose wounds don't ask for so much blood.

11

SPARRING WITH BRUNO

During the period of training solo and moving between gyms, I hired myself out for sparring throughout Europe. The first big job as a sparring partner was with Frank Bruno. We fought daily under a blue training marquee, erected just for his benefit behind a health spa. It contained a boxing ring, a small stage with three or four punchbags suspended on invisible threads of rope, a stair-master, a medicine ball and floor mats. Although I was a supporter of Bruno, as I stood before him all I saw was a man. He was of flesh and bone, built like a warrior. No, built like several fighters all equal in size. Like a mountain on top of another mountain and set against the sky. Even in slow motion his right and left came through like ramrods. Bruno cast a strong and silent shadow. He was like an ancient darkness that turned the sky black on me. All that lit my way were the million flashing stars of the photographers. While we stood I could see the lightning piling up in his twitching muscles. He looked confident with all the conditioning of his training. He came over to me one day after a session and told me to go down if I got hurt and take the time to clear my head. But I didn't remember Bruno ever going down to take the time to clear his head. Once he got hurt he stayed hurt.

Physical fitness and talent is never enough. After years of facing opponents the fight had already broken the certainty of cause and effect embedded in Bruno's mind. He lacked the killer instinct. If he hit you, you were supposed to fall. If you didn't he would step back and re-evaluate everything he thought he knew. This is what happened in his first Tyson fight, against Bone Crusher Smith and also against Lennox Lewis. I think he could have beaten them all.

I soon realised that I was allowing him to rule triumphant. I grew tired while breathing his stale and eroded air but I held together better than he anticipated. The souls of two warriors rose and met under that tent. For me these were hungry times that would be forgotten in the future after strong bodies had ceased to function. Stone statues came face to face. His trainer, George Francis, whispered instructions before leaving enclosed fighters to wander in circles around their spheres. He tried to take the centre but I opposed him.

I chose to stand and fight, not to run and hide. What could he prove? Suddenly he seemed vulnerable, yet courage drove him. He had heart and that's what everyone liked about him. This was our destiny and because of it our corpses would fall. But in which canvas would we drown abandoned? After the search for our bodies, what would they find among our violent fires? Men without faces? Mouths that have no way with words? Who will decipher the fire burning in our souls without substance, pure nonsense? Who has the wisdom of someone who knows nothing? Bruno wanted to be a fighter, wanted to have something to cherish. Something he could look back on and know that it wasn't all a dream.

The crudest contest sees men circling one another like prowling animals. Yet it is sold to the masses as a noble art, when in reality it's just a living for noble warriors. Our bones may become visible though they were not meant to be seen. I'd watched Bruno closely from the beginning of his journey for what he may have achieved. Economically secure, he now stands defiant having shed his slave skin. He took his opportunity well and walked home in glory with his pride and a championship belt. I worked with Bruno for three of his fights. Our sessions were watched by television personalities and footballers who came to be pampered with mud baths, massages and facials to name but a few indulgences. They would ask stupid questions such as, 'Are you really trying to hurt each other?'

There were sparring sessions for the media but promoter Mickey Duff wouldn't allow our sparring sessions to be seen. I was ranked third or fourth in the country at the time so I understood he wouldn't have wanted the media to have seen me getting the better of Bruno. Mickey Duff chose fat, overweight Americans for Bruno to beat up for the British public. How does Bruno cope without the fight that defined him? There is a solitude in the ring but it still pulls us in. There is a thirst and a hunger and we are its fruit. There are victories and defeats, and fighting men are those things' miracles.

I remember the first time I entered the ring for sparring. I wore trainers instead of boxing boots. After training Bruno asked me why. I explained that I only had one pair and needed them to fight in. The next day he gave me a new pair of boots. I asked if I could use his skipping rope. The next day I was given a rope. I asked to use his bag gloves. The next day I was given gloves. He gave me T-shirts, shorts and a pair of signed boxing gloves for my son Cassius. Bruno is a nice guy.

I admired the courage it took for him to meet iron times with iron fists. But he must have been listening to the whispers of his inner voice, recognised its sounds and traced its origin to doubt. He already knew the practised ways of survival. He had developed as a boxer through a profound and instinctive understanding of nature's laws. Iron Mike Tyson had a rhythmic routine and gave ritual beatings with the purpose of a battle-drum advancing between the howls of his furious intent. I remember seeing the agony that gripped the face of Frank Bruno's wife as she watched him falling into the ropes while Tyson hit him repeatedly with sickening uppercuts. I also remember the quiet smiles of the opposite corner, Tyson's people. Did Bruno know what he already had? Pressed against the ropes, the reality relentlessly crowding in, the pressure, size and savage appearance of a harbour shark communicated itself to him above water, all his thoughts swallowed by desire. The moment was lost, opportunity would not be seen again. His was just another dream washed away with the tide of time.

I once saw a homeless man making a bed from cardboard boxes beneath the night sky, safe from an uncaring world though not secure from crawling hunger. I watched him lying on his improvised bed with no sign of displeasure and with a certain delight on his face while looking up at the stars that lit his tedious appetite. I approached him and offered him money that he refused. We spoke for a while and I thought as we spoke, 'He knows something, but what, I wonder? Why can't I see the stars as well through my eyes as he does through his?'

Does anyone really know or understand the thing that ties one star to the next? He explained to me that he was bound everywhere he looked on earth by hostile perimeters, except above. To him the earth was a monster of energy, eternal, self-creating, an apparent planet. He woke in the midst of Mother Earth's dream and realised he was dreaming but, unable to wake, he continued dreaming, witnessing her chaos, and her power, her beauty and Nature's wisdom. This is an ambiguous place, knowledgeable and unknowing, with no meaning and countless meanings. He knew that if counted, calculated and expressed in formulaes, how could she be comprehended as the work of art that gave birth to herself? Man strives to become master over her body, to extend his own power, to dominate her and grow stronger. He sucks the blood from her jugular with penetrating fangs to feed his machines with their poisonous breath. He knows that one day the giant Earth will be forced to defend herself against his ego. She will demonstrate her incomprehensible force, her true power, defeat his vanity and bring him to his knees. Through a night sky he seemed to understand the horror and absurdity of our actions and through that space he saw art. The expert healer had covered with a veil of beauty his visions of horror and painted for himself an open sky without boundaries. He was an intelligent man wanting nothing. I thought he was homeless but I was wrong. He'd turned his back on us, away from our foolishness, our materialism. The earth was his home.

I received a good-luck note in my dressing room from Bruno on the night I fought Herbie Hide for the British Title. We shared the same likes and dislikes for Hide. The fight had been on the cards for a while but I was given two weeks' notice for the fight. Even though I was still getting over a flu virus I felt that I could beat Hide with two minutes' notice. On the night of the fight my senses rushed inwards and shrank beneath a dark cloud of infection.

We were two boys who obeyed violence to gratify our unknown senses, while dragging the chains of our lives in weary hunger and murderous thoughts. We assumed our power, dictated swift fists and without fear unfolded our obscure vision. The unseen darkness was measured punch by punch and the hour was divided round by round. We strove in battle, in an accepted conflict with our revolving shapes, silent in our activity. I never saw the final punch and it left behind a self-contemplating shadow occupied with an enormous labour. The draught of light drew confusion into my indefinite space. I was forced to tend to my once roaring flames, that I might quench my own despair. I had to locate the centre where, if suspended, I could stand and throw a stone into the dismal abyss to measure out my ordered space. Then I could find the one who was counting the fingers that divided my fallen time. I was alone, but the words 'What are you doing on the floor?' filtered through my contracted senses. I knew that I would survive to tell the tale, and that Hide could not put out the eternal fire burning inside me, but self-pity divided my heart and soul as I climbed to my feet and the referee waved off the fight.

A fool sees what he wants to see and unless the sun shines on him he will never become a star. Bruno was a star, the sun was shining and the nation loved him but he put aside good advice and found the pride to defend his title.

12

A NEW LIFE

Armed with razor-sharp knuckles of flesh and bone, consenting men murder notions of violence with precision and clarity of direction. They rise above gravity to sharpen their hands, sense of time, rhythm, things that set muscle to motion. Boxers are perfect fighting animals governed by instincts, attuned to their environment and able to act without conscious thought. Able to act without seeing themselves in an analytical mirror. They fight, man versus man, in front of an audience. They battle each other with pride and vanity's howling agony, like endangered animals forced to abandon their element. Hunters, masters of that wave made up of a million bodies and one head, they choose to fight because they were born to fight. Enemies share the same heartbeat, the same pain, the same dry lips invaded by thirst and hunger. They are consumed by the fire of a phantom-filled inner world. They do battle because the fight was born in the blood, all too often nurtured in sunburnt bodies by the hard lives of dead fathers.

Fighters are often treated like a herd of human cattle endlessly used to fill bottomless pockets that can never be filled. The meat comes cheap from boys who have suffered poverty, race and class hate. It is easily replaced. The men known as promoters live in mansions surrounded by barbed wire fences, iron gates and security cameras. They eat off spotless plates while their stables overflow with prize fighters. These men drag their spirits like a briefcase full of old wounds and are, by choice, immune to pity and whatever moans you or I may have. Society cannot protect us from the greed it creates in us. I climb through the ropes and expect gold for my blood. What price should be paid for knocking a man unconscious and watching the canvas become red with his bleeding heart? It seems that somewhere along the line the ends got mixed up with the means. In the end most fighters lose, and defeat is made worse because they have no way to express it. I know the sighs of men that have no skill to speak of their distress, no way to describe their will or imagination.

It's a way of life which puzzles and repulses many people, because they don't understand the motivations. Yesterday I met a man who looked at my hands in daylight and said he knew my story but couldn't understand why I boxed. They weren't the hands of a man who made a conventional living; they were hard with sharpened knuckles.

He asked me a very cold and deliberate question. 'Could you live the rest of your life without ever punching another human being in the face?'

I'd never seen this man before and if I never see him again that would be fine by me. I looked him in the eyes and asked him, 'How wonderful is your life, when nothing matters more than anything else? In whom or what lies your passion, where's your love and what would you do for that love? And besides, this is the track my life was set on and it stretches in front of me without end.'

He turned away from me, put his hands in his pockets and walked away.

Hard necessity drives us to sever heads with our sharpened hands. Why not try to sleep tonight and forget for a few hours? You know that you could be woken by the sound of your head being tossed over my shoulder, or with the news of your own death or maybe the death of someone you knew who'd simply been hungry and fought to eat without success. How will your head appear to you, torn from your shoulders, perfectly cut? I wish for all that you have. Close your eyes and count to ten or leave them open and watch your head disappear. Be quiet! I'll wipe my hands on your shirt and leave before you even reach ten. In the morning you can tell the story of how you wanted me gone, how you wanted me to disappear and never to come back. If I lose my head who feeds my family? Believe me, I will be back if it takes your head to do so.

By June Angela was pregnant again. Caution crept into our hearts and stayed there, motionless, meditating for nine months. A thought was frozen but clear. A memory remained of a minute, an hour, a year when red blood flooded every sense in an explosion of foetal fluids. My heart almost became too heavy from the fall-out. Raindrops, a few drops fell on my face and on my eyes and I thought I saw the whole picture. Each struggle contains a light, a small illuminated act. Love's image is made from the scattered pictures of those moments, those fragments that the mind holds on to and draws together. After the wait I raised my head, and love had pushed up through my heart. Her eyes were brown. Chiara Juanita, who are you that came from my seed and grew from your mother's womb? Were you born with hope?

I remember the day I met you, the day it became impossible to separate myself from you, the day our hearts fused and began beating as one. It all happened in the dark. Your chest moves in rhythmic waves, you live, you breath by swallowing. I felt your tiny feet and smooth soft skin. I took your hand without saying a word. You slept, your mother cried, for finally she had the baby girl she always wanted. She gazed at you and sat smugly in admiration of herself. A new part of us that she had created. We watched you grow an inch at a time, like watching a flower. Watching a new life bud and grow, waiting for petals to appear. The stem grew thicker, the cautious roots reached through to each of us. Finally, beautiful flower, you bloomed, demanding that the sun and the moon pay enough attention and properly appreciate you. We share your discoveries and witness you falling, endlessly falling. Will you ever stop falling? I know you will continue falling into the night and day, into movement and stillness, into liveliness, into life.

A new life was not the only family matter I had to deal with. My son Cassius came home from school upset and told me of an English teacher, a substitute. He had sat with his feet upon the desk, attempting a pretence of knowledge. The teacher shouted across the classroom at my son, saying he should get something into his thick black head. Cass and a classmate protested. He then punished them both with a detention for answering back. I was prompted to write the following letter to the Headmaster:

Dear Sir,
RE: CASSIUS MURRAY
Cassius came home from school on Tuesday and informed me that one of his teachers had shouted across the classroom that he should get something into his thick black head. After I spoke to the Deputy Head the teacher in question phoned me. He told me that he had never said black and insisted that his words were simply 'thick head', that this was in front of the whole class and no one heard the word black. I accepted his explanation of the event. However, let's examine the words 'thick head':

THICK, having a relatively large distance between opposite sides, or a specified distance. Large diameter. Containing a lot of solid matter, viscous. Difficult to see through. (Of speech) not clear. (Of a person) stupid.

THICK-HEAD, a stupid person, unable to think clearly for whatever reason. Thickness, the state, quality or degree of being thick[1].

Unfortunately, Cassius is not thick-skinned. He is a very sensitive boy. At home I don't allow any hitting or name-calling between siblings. Nor the use of derogatory words about each other's intelligence. I am sure that you can appreciate that the effects of such words can be far reaching. It is possible that there could be children suffering from dyslexia in the class. Words like 'thick head' could seriously damage their confidence.

Words like these are inappropriate in the classroom.

Yours faithfully,

M. Murray

[1] Chambers Pocket Dictionary.

Malcom X said, 'Only a fool would allow his children to be educated by his enemy.' But I don't think it's as simple as one enemy. When we fight ignorance in the education system, we're fighting an enemy with one body but two heads: one hates difference and discriminates against it; the other ignores the idea of difference and calls discrimination a figment of our imaginations. Both affect my children's education. Perhaps a fellow boxer, Joe Louis, had the answer when he said, 'Kill the body and the head will fall.'

The fire in me was conceived in hungry silence, and lives on in furious hands. This could burn until the end, carried like an Olympic torch, passed to the young hearts of my kids without sound, hand to hand, without pain or economic considerations in search of glory. But remember, kids, that eternity is not yours and the stage is set for you to give your heart or have it taken away. There's no time to lose. They are already writing a cheque in your names.

This is what I urge my children to do. Sharpen your eyes with an optimistic view. Come from beneath your shells and experience the cold shudder that awakens you to bright day. Stretch out your arms into the warm air that breaths beneath your fingers and look around you. Believe you're alive. Go for glory and be aware of those who will try to break and poison your minds with doubt. Disregard them. Awaken to the goodness of those who make you smile and reveal to you their trust. To an enemy show no weakness. Feel the moment. Life is short whether the rain comes down or the days are sunny, whether it's the cold of winter or the heat of summer. When you dream in your youth remember, wise men or fools, you're young and the future is yours, be inspired. One day you will be old and all that you know will be forgotten and only recalled in the ashes of a dream's memory. Leave the wise and learned to discuss the world until their mouths are stopped with dust. Know one thing is certain – your lives. I've listened to great arguments about life and death, God, the soul and many other things. All presented by men too heavy to drive their knowledge beyond their own time and too afraid to create eyes for themselves to survey millenniums. If they did, then where would their theories be? One by one they would have crept silently to rest. Make the most of your one certainty . . . life.

13

STOCKPORT GYM

One night my rising and falling arm, my right arm, popped out of its socket and hung free from my control by a thread. Pain like that has a way of remembering itself. Its vision lasts indefinitely. With the help of ringside doctors I didn't have to be brave. I got the morphine I needed to stop the pain and that enabled them to pop the arm back without my fussing. Bravery is a question of holding out. Some can hold out longer than others but sooner or later they all give in to pain. It's definitely not a question of fear or of being afraid. What made my horror even worse was the fact that it was not the first time I'd dislocated the same shoulder. Does destiny take pleasure in repetition?

The morphine brought an endless and flooded dreamland. I found there the man (or beast) who always wore black and lived in shadows. All I could see of him was his teeth, but that was enough to bring a cold sweat. This simple, serious and strong shadow was my father. He brought me to the street where we had lived and showed me violent memories. I threatened him, tried to make him speak, but he said nothing. The scene shifted and we faced each other in a boxing ring. Our bloodied faces faded and blurred as four hands exploded with pain. The echoing shouts dimmed into a mist of darkness. The final punch forced my detached lips to taste the canvas. It opened its mouth and I fell into its watery depths. But when it tried to swallow the man that had knocked me out, it choked and spat him back into waves of applause. The referee was too fat with his supper and couldn't keep up with our movements, so he splashed and played in the puddles of sweat and blood and after the fight he just continued to sing and dance in my blood.

I had dislocated my shoulder three times and each time I went through the same process. First I drowned my sorrows. I threw clenched notes towards the barman, who sold me a plausible emptiness. Misery loves company, and all too often the barman would join me, sharing the fact that he'd wished away the soreness of his unimpressive life. I listened to him for a while, drank more Guinness then dragged myself home.

Then I would cast aside doubt and all that wasn't inspiration. I would ignore the idiots who questioned but never got the answers they wanted to hear. They'd just plot when and how to ask me the same disguised questions. The publishers of doubt and despair. The scientists who smiled with condescension after telling me that my fighting days were no more. The divided image by which I defined myself hung in the balance. In response, I cleared my forehead to enlarge my mind, and the window of perception opened.

As I saw it there were three possible solutions to the shoulder problem. The first was negative, nothing special happening for me in the world of boxing. I could've given up. The second was an operation, cutting, stitching and plaiting the muscles together which would've put me out of the ring for a long time, possibly forever. The third was the most plausible. I would rebuild the shoulder muscles and carry on. I joined a weightlifting gym in Stockport. It was full of weight machines and free weights, not forgetting the sun beds and walls of mirrors, because after all this was a bodybuilding gym. I became an expert on the shoulder joint, the most complicated of all joints. The knee, elbow and other joints are limited in their movement but the shoulder can rotate and is free to move in any direction. I had to build the front, rear and side muscles, and the top also, with shoulder-pressing exercises.

I met different characters in the gym, though mainly bodybuilders. Ugly people weren't allowed through these doors. You couldn't be fat. You had to be beautiful. Plastic men and women everywhere. Nothing was real. Together but isolated they trained, fulfilling nothing. Taking everything for granted but themselves. Busy people escaping from what was on their minds. After training and wiping the trickles of sweat from their brows, where did they go? Back to their offices full of energy for what? Vanity!

There was one guy called Matthew. He looked fit, with plenty of muscles on his bones and growing from his ears. He had a very well-built body that attracted the attention of all who saw him. He always left the gym in a purring convertible without worry of rain, with manicured hands, an eye-catching suit and expensive shoes that covered his feet. You couldn't help but notice his biceps. So what if his head was filled with nothing.

He lived in the city with his wife and no kids. Day and night he lifted weights to build his body to fulfil his plans of perfection. Matthew pumped iron in the silence of a crowded gym where he was only aware of himself, endlessly checking the contours of his body in a full-length mirror. After all that work, he must have woken one night to discover his body had turned to stone, a perfect statue. He was a happy man whose dreams had come true. He still lives in the city with his wife, but after years of steroid abuse, a low sperm count and no kids. He's unable to lift weights with one kidney, breasts, a failing liver and a variety of other complaints. Day and night he lifted weights to build his body, to fulfil his marble plan.

I rebuilt my shoulder and left that gym in Stockport to train once again in a boxing gym with real people who sweat, spit, bleed and break wind while training without upsetting anyone. Before I got back to boxing I had to go for my annual compulsory MOT, an MRI brain scan. The smallest irregularity would cost you your licence.

My brain was still there. A chest X-ray: my heart and lungs still functioned. Eye test: 20-20 vision. Hearing worked, if you spoke up. No broken bones at that time. HIV test: negative. Hepatitis jabs? Yes, I'd had those. Blood pressure lowish. Water sample all clear. Balance and limb movement fine. No allergies or diseases ran in the family. I was a perfect human specimen, as always.

14

MR TRICKETT

I looked long and hard over my past, my uncertain future, and accepted the arrival of an inevitable moment when I'd see myself. At that point, I would become conscious of me, then lose myself in the clarity of the moment. I felt like an empty space in a meat market: a shadow with no one to box. All my life I'd lived between the rules other people made. I'd created a character I couldn't separate myself from: someone who'd searched for the discerning audience that could distinguish between a pretender and a contender. I was ready to fight on request and show my passion for the game to anyone interested. Promoters and managers had grown fat on the blood of our wounds but still they whistled and I'd come running. I'm not a dog, but I was willing to save their promotions for fear of missing my opportunity before this body crumbled into dust.

Centuries ago, someone forced men to fight and called it sport. He must have needed the stench of blood or the sight of men running to entertain him. Some fought back like wild men, avoiding death and winning their freedom. They became heroes, warriors, gladiators who took from the fight what they needed to live. I can identify with those men. Every day at 5 p.m. I leave home with my gym bag and head towards the gym accompanied by the need to avoid pain, which is the need to make a better life. There is and always will be a need to fight. What about the need to do something that hasn't been done already? Some guys train hard, setting themselves the tasks of winning. Others do something, maybe a little training here, or a little run there. I say do anything, do whatever, only be proud. You will not forget the events in your life when pride is part of those things, but you will regret the events when pride walked out of the door.

My manager, Jack Trickett, owner of a hotel and a former fighter himself, has a great job. He merely picks up the phone and wastes time talking. He wears nice suits and looks professional, but don't let that fool you. He doesn't recall ring-work at all. Though he works hard at his other job. He's always off somewhere doing something else. Isn't he supposed to get me fights? Phil Martin disliked Jack, he resented the fact that he did most of the work as a trainer and only received 10 per cent whilst as a manager Jack got 25 per cent. Phil wanted to manage all who trained at his camp, to reap the harvest and be given all the praise. He'd warned me about Jack's trickery, though Mr Trickett had always been straight with me. Phil called him ambitious and greedy – talk about the pot calling the kettle black. He asked me to sign a contract with him but I refused and stayed with Jack. Some of the other fighters signed.

Jack's nickname on the street is Tricky Dicky. But my grandmother always told me to take everyone you meet as you find them. I always found him to be honest and I respected him. Honesty is truly a rare commodity in the boxing business. Why shouldn't he be ambitious? All he wants is a World Champion. Can everything we want be obtained with money? Many people have tried to fuck him over, but Jack knows what he knows after more than half a century in the business and that makes it difficult to pull the wool over his eyes.

Jack rang me in October of 1995. 'It's a twelve-rounder in Munich next week against Zeljko Mavrovic, the European Champion. I know you've not been in the gym much but it's decent money. Do you want it?'

I turned to my wife, who gives me the look that I've become familiar with over the years. In the gym or not I better take the fight. In her words, 'I want to go shopping!' I took the fight. That's my job.

'You'll have to be careful with this guy.' He warned me, 'He's a strong, dangerous bastard. Tuck up tight, use a good jab and don't get hurt.'

Jack got back to what he does best, looking for an angle. His preoccupation is always with finding a loophole, and he's always convinced it must be somewhere. I told him, 'Jack, focus, get me more money!'

That's all Jack can do for me. I think he knows it too because, by fight night, Jack always looks in a state of controlled panic. The world would be a mist and then a minute later it was vast and clear. The trainers are there to tell us how, though I'd lost all faith in them. The cut-men are there if we need them during a fight but what can a manager do for us after the ringing of the bell? Maybe they could find a way to help if fighters gave them half a chance.

There can be no rest for me. Somewhere near, fear sharpens the hands of my opponents. The ring has been built and is being lowered into a dark arena as I write. Matchmakers are on the lookout to find themselves a mug. Should I be afraid? I know that when I'm not ready, the phone always rings asking for my hand a day or two before, to face sharpened teeth and hungry fists. Okay, why not? I know what's concealed behind handfuls of cash and greedy eyes. 'Come on, don't worry, you can beat this kid,' they'll tell me. How stupid do they think I am? I know their game but as it happens I can beat their boy. But they don't know that. No rest, they'll be knocking on my dressing room door before you know it saying, 'It's time.' The ring was built to contain rage as a pan contains boiling water. So the canvas absorbs a fighter's fresh blood. This is not a place for the faint-hearted, nor is it a place where souls are violated. This is a space for hardened individuals, inviolable, consenting.

The battle's aftermath presents no regrets for having fought. Here a human being can be chopped down, gutted, enslaved by pain or dreams of glory. Scattered hopes upturned or abandoned by the fallen are all casualties of the game. All their stories are printed on the surface of used canvas. Fighters leave their blood and sweat, spit, water or anything else that a well-placed punch to the stomach can bring up, on a stained floor. Bright lights sharpen the mind's focus. Hands and eyes perform their function with cunning, predicting the sly, swift movements of shadowed hit men wearing gloved axes. Like lions, they circle with patience laying their traps, slipping in and out of pain to land a hunter's prize. We pour ourselves into the centre of our agreement, knowing that blood will flow from the wounds we inflict on each other. One day all our hearts will stop beating, but until then sharpened hands shaped by society will file themselves against consenting heads, for a piece of gold. I would like to say to hell with the future, knowing that our future lies at the centre of pain, floating on pools of blood between four ropes. No one hesitates to crack open your head and turn from you with raised hands into applause.

Doesn't life write the contract that binds us together as eager warriors, driven by our needs and those of our families? Life sees us roaring through the night with fractured hands, cursing one another. Our circumstances throw us together, leaving us with just a hostile glimpse of the moment in which we truly live. I am one body severed by two fists. I think with my instincts as well as my hands, without conscious thought. Think of a fighter without seeing the stereotype and maybe you can learn to love me without judgement. Sometimes I feel sad because I enjoy it so much, but the reality is that I fight, and that expresses a physical need to follow my destiny. There is a place in this noble art that allows me to live simply, without retreating into hiding, afraid of the turmoil the world offers me. How should I live? How do you live? If you are going to think about it, try not to think too much.

Remember we know nothing and we are strangers, however we live. Just try to be everything you can be. Put all that you are into everything you do and fortune will be granted.

THE JOURNEYMAN

15

DENMARK

I've tried to fill my glove-shaped heart high with bank notes, but waiting is a way of life for fighters scratching a living from the ring's painful dream. There has always been a certain poetry to a fight when the ring turns into a stage, a single play that enacts the rage of two human beings. That's what I loved and that's what I had to focus on. While waiting for the fight in Munich I decided to travel to Denmark to work with a fighter called Brian Neilson.

Brian had won a Super-heavyweight Bronze medal in the 1992 Barcelona Olympics and was at the time as big a hero in his country as Frank Bruno was in ours. He was unbeaten and chasing Rocky Marciano's 49–0 streak. He met me at the airport, introduced himself in broken English and walked me to his car. He drove like a maniac, but that wasn't the worst thing about being in a car with him. He filled the car with his own gas. If I'd put a match to the air, it would have burned. It hovered over our heads like a mist. The question I asked myself was 'Is it going to stink?' It did, and I began to choke. God knows what he had eaten. I swallowed and wound down the window. The fire in his belly must have been raging. He found the whole ordeal amusing. Clearly he wasn't a man interested in making a good first impression. He didn't. The conversation was simple . . . boxing. He took me straight to the gym. I knew their plan. Brian introduced me to his trainer, who didn't beat about the bush. 'Can you do eight rounds today? Today we do eight rounds.'

There was the plan. Book me on an early morning flight. Meet me at the airport. Drive me for an hour and a half to the gym, then jump on me for eight rounds. Brian was already in the centre of the gym getting changed. I looked around the gym and Brian seemed to fill it all by himself. He was big but it wasn't muscle. Folds of flesh overlapped his belly. I took one look and thought, 'If he can do eight rounds then so can I.'

He surprised me. He was tough and relished the pleasure of an absolute war. I knew what the question was. Could I fight? If that answer had been no, I can't, I would've been on the next plane home. I couldn't believe I'd allowed myself to be thrown into that type of gym war for peanuts. I'd sparred all over the world and knew that a sparring partner does only enough. You see, if you're being paid you don't beat up the guy whose paying you because you'll be sent home for being too good. If you let him beat you up his trainer will send you home for not being good enough. Either way will leave you out of pocket. After the training, we left the gym and drove out to a very nice home that belonged to his sponsor, a locksmith. He had a wife and two lovely kids. The kids spoke no English and called me Mickey Mouse.

Who understands a heavyweight's appetite better than another heavyweight? After sparring I needed a piece of meat. 'Brian, if I don't eat soon I'll go and find a cow myself. What's that smell? Oh no, you haven't . . . '

He'd burnt my steak and thrown it in the bin along with the vegetables. The nearest shop was ten miles away and possibly closed. I asked him where he'd put the bin bags and that maybe we could retrieve something before the rats crawled out dragging their bellies. We searched the rotten sacks with flashlights in the dark at the back of the house. I looked at him as I brought my fingers to my nose to smell the stink on my hands. He looked away. He wanted to say something but didn't dare.

I was in training camp far away from home and beginning to understand how it was possible to be in one place, willing to do anything to be somewhere else. After weeks in training camp, strangers were now friends. Trainers taught us how to slip right hands. Listen to the experts! Every morning I woke from a warm bed to rain, wind and a cold frost, to run the streets of Denmark step by step. I was confined for weeks in camp with freedom on the other side of conscious pain. I focused on dark shadows with familiar shoulders able to move at the speed of light. We shared in hard times and understood the reasons why.

I sparred hundreds of rounds with Neilson as he prepared for his fight with Bone Crusher Smith. Smith was one of the first men to have gone the distance with Iron Mike Tyson and the first man to have beaten our own Frank Bruno. 'Neilson has fast hands,' whispered his trainer and I believed him. Arrogant shadows boasted they were faster than their origins. When I was younger I didn't think it possible. 'Faster, faster,' said the trainer but my brain worked slower and slower, trying to cope with sore feet and blood that moved at funeral pace. When did I become old?

How did Brian Neilson get so far in this game? He ate and his hunger grew with eating. He smoked cigarettes and made me promise not to tell. He never ran. His only training was sparring eight or ten rounds a day and they were always a war. In training each day is the same as the next. After training we would eat and sit around watching videos. We watched a man standing in front of Michael McCallum, the Body Snatcher, leaning forward protecting his ribcage thinking, 'If only my body was invisible, punches couldn't find me, and I might not be dumped on the floor of this ring, searching for air.'

We saw a cocky kid who thought he could conquer the world with his fists. After leaving school with nothing except the ability to write his name, what was his choice? He fought for the sheer

THE JOURNEYMAN

pleasure of it and he took the time to plan carefully his direction in life. His path took him through a list of fighters he'd beaten to be crowned king. He was a kid who found the focus to fight his way out of the cage he was born to. Known as The Prince, he had fought his first professional fight against Ricky Beard on a bill I topped in Mansfield.

It was an eliminator for the British Heavyweight title, which was then vacant. I was to contest that title with the Norwich based ex-WBO Champion, Herbie Hide, a former sparring partner. It was organised on only a week's notice by Frank Warren. I remember Riddick Bowe, at the time Heavyweight Champion of the World, slept ringside because of a long flight from the States. However, Naseem stole the show. He knew first hand what it was like to stand face to face with an opponent and put him down for the count.

All this viewing of classic fights reminded me of the great boxers. We watched as the dancing master Willie Pep moved as light-footed as Fred Astaire. He danced fight after fight until he got caught by a black kid with dynamite in his hands. He slammed into the kid's gloves and jammed against his knuckles. His head was nearly torn from his neck. His jaw must have been in fragments. His face was as bruised and swollen as if he had been beaten by a hundred fists. With his nose still bleeding after the bout he remained wide-eyed and smiling. The cameras kept on filming this brave dancing master who had nothing to prove to anyone.

We watched a documentary called *The 64 Day Hero,* which told the story of Randolf Turpin. He was a middleweight that people came from all around to watch. They wanted to see the man that took the title from the great Sugar Ray Robinson. Every man wanted to be him and have the money and the glory that came with a world title. At the end of 64 days the Sugar Man came back and took that which belonged to him, the belt. The hero was no longer a hero. When the money went so did the friends, but I still don't know why the ex-champion put a shotgun into his mouth and blew his brains out. I thought he was a fighter!

Muhammad Ali was the greatest sporting personality I ever saw. A great human being and my hero. But pound for pound the greatest fighter I've ever seen was Sugar Ray Robinson. His record was 85–0 before he lost his first fight. There was something in the way he twisted and moved, throwing lightning combinations, and the way he turned the light out on opponents, elegantly sending them into darkness. There was something in the way he fought against fatigue as the rounds quietly passed into one another, listening only to an inner voice that told him to ignore the bright lights that shone only for him and trust his feet. 'You can't fall, just feel the rhythm.' Something too in the way he fed men sugar-coated knuckles, then tap danced to the sweet purr of his pink Cadillac. There was just something about the Sugar Man that reached inside me, like the sound of a great flamenco guitar with its rhythms, its passion and the joy for the moment it truly lives.

What work and last are the fundamentals you start with. Take the jab and the right cross, the one-two, making sure that your body weight is evenly distributed. After throwing the right hand, come back with a left hook and that will correct your balance. Your hands should be high and your chin down. Eye contact should always be maintained with elbows tucked in to protect the ribcage. Stay within punching range but keep an arm's length distant. If you roll under a hook do not look at the floor or you will not see the uppercut. Hold the centre of the ring and don't get caught with your back against the ropes. Take the basics from an older fighter and you will open the defence of a young fighter. These are some of the fundamentals a coach teaches an amateur, but, believe me, if he can't fight they'll be useless against a boxer who can. I had no amateur experience. I was unpractised in the ways of the ring. My heart was fashioned in the skill of pain management and I believed, and still believe, that a man or a woman can either fight or they can't. No amount of training or teaching will stick in the vacant minds of confused people seeking shade in the heat of battle. Their instincts will survey the consequence of the conflicts close at hand, confirming and justifying their fears. If they are fighters their instincts will make them oblivious to all this. Without instinct a fighter would be nothing, living eternity in the spell of one truth, in a perspective that makes what is close at hand appear as the reality of his worst imaginings. He would be ignorant to the fact that conflicts have many truths, perspectives and relative interpretations.

Brian and I shared many moments in Copenhagen, moments that passed before us when neither he nor I would quit. Neilson recently met the Iron Man, Mike Tyson, perceived by the public as an animal or a kind of brutish human who likes to hurt people. Not because of his job, but because on several occasions he'd forgotten how to be a gentleman.

As for biting off part of a Evander Holyfield's ear, although a brutish act, I understand perhaps why Tyson did it. I fought a guy in Cardiff called Keith Fletcher from Bristol. After having just dropped him with a right hand, when I was moving in for the finish he grabbed me and tried to bite my shoulder but was unable to get a firm grip. When I wobbled him with another punch he rugby tackled me through the ropes. I almost broke my back falling out of the ring. We continued the fight and the moment I hurt him he grabbed me once again but this time he spat out his gum-shield and took a chunk of flesh from my neck. He drew a lot of blood. He was thrown out and disqualified. My first thought was 'coward'! Rather than get knocked out he got himself thrown out. This was all after having to be restrained at the weigh-in, growling and spitting aggression and telling everyone how he was going to tear me apart. Now I realise that beyond human eyes there is a stress our senses cannot penetrate and if left unchecked it can torment the soul with monstrous consequences. The solitary nature and strain of a boxing ring can restrict our perceptions and have the power to drive a man to dark despair and breakdown. Our wars are also the wars of life.

Brian met Tyson in Copenhagen's Parken, a 40,000-seat stadium. It was a huge night for Danish boxing. The fight was lost before it began. As always, men are overwhelmed by time but the earth keeps its infinity. Neilson's best day was many years behind him and Tyson's people knew it, despite Neilson's 61–1 record and him being the only heavyweight to have eclipsed Rocky Marciano's 49-fight winning streak. The audience in attendance marked unnecessary score cards then closed their eyes to Tyson's naked rage. Neilson quivered with concussion shock each time Tyson landed a punch. His legs shuddered, each muscle in convulsions as knuckles smashed endlessly against his head. The Danish fans watched the flesh stripped from his ribcage. The fight was an act of fierce desire, blinding Neilson's reason with the lust for more youth. The warrior's spirit still lived in him. He felt the bravery renewing itself and the desire of ancient times continued to burn in his belly. Only Tyson could stem the fire that consumed him. A self-renewed 17 st rebel, Tyson bobbed and rolled under Neilson's leathered combinations. His rebellious eyes were fixed without compromise in his face. He devoured Neilson round after round, the ring lights illuminating Neilson's punishing opponent. There was no shelter from Tyson's thunder. His forehead roared towards the prize and obscured Neilson's vision. After seven rounds Neilson refused to renew his torment and quit on his stool, denying Tyson and the public his head, along with the opportunity to quench their thirst and subdue their hunger. Wisdom like that can't be measured by the hourglass.

I cannot guess the reason why time passes at a certain speed but it was time to go home. I knew when I was finished training with Neilson. There was nothing more I could do. I was ready.

16

MUNICH

I flew back to Manchester airport and was met by my wife and kids. I had one day at home, just enough time to pack a bag before flying off to Germany. I was accompanied by my new trainer, Bob Shannon. Bob was a nervous flyer who crossed himself on the way up and held on tight on the way down. When the pilot spoke I'm sure Bob heard something different. Something along the lines of 'Ladies and gentlemen, we are about to begin our descent. Please fasten your seat belts and pray to your God. If you don't have one, now would be a good time to get one.'

We finally arrived in Munich. We were met and taken to a very nice hotel. My manager, Jack Trickett, was in the hotel lobby, where other managers and promoters sat drinking coffee, nervously discussing confidential nothings with each other and their boxers. The world, suddenly so remote from anything rational, revolved around a few simple necessities before the awaited fight. It's moments like these when I recognise the cause and the wisdom of teaching strong bodies to support themselves. The wisdom was to be learnt right there where life was in the moment.

We found a table and sat for a while and had some lunch. It was a very large meal. We sat there until boredom got the better of me and I went to look for a driver who could take me out and show me a little of Germany. I told everyone I'd see them later at the weigh-in and set off to see the sights. We drove for a while and I had no idea where we were. The driver spoke very little English. He drove us to a large field that looked like farmers' land and tried to explain to me that it used to be a battlefield. After several minutes and hand gestures he understood that I wanted him to wait while I walked off my lunch.

I searched for my spirit on that old battlefield where the ghosts of dead warriors who lived and died were free: men who carried swords, axes and lances into war. It's a miracle they still live on in memory. Imagine if not even a shadow of these spirits who gave their hearts and souls was left. I felt watched and ashamed to have forgotten their wars. Battlefields today look as if nothing happened. I walked through a very pretty meadow so well painted that it couldn't make you sad. The colours were bright, lots of flowers and, a blue sky with few clouds. There was a tree full of green leaves and, underneath, a big rock that shone in the sun. A headless lizard ran in circles looking for its brains, avoiding a puddle of blood. I stepped over him, checking my own head was still intact. A farmer with a bull and a dog running next to him peacefully ploughed the land where the ghosts of dead warriors live. Birds glided through still skies avoiding the bullets of hunters. Some fell and had their heads chopped off. Jets of blood burst from their necks and spilt onto the ground like red waterfalls. No bird pitied or cried for itself. I imagined that at night, when the field was alone, it remembered all the dead. It would cry and water the flowers with blood that still hadn't stop running, until angels came down and made each warrior whole. I was at peace in a place where men witnessed humanity's death with their own eyes and did nothing.

There were two dozen of us weighing in on the eve of battle. As usual, lively arguments were going on amongst trainers, managers and promoters: weight; money; the order of bouts; hotels and whatever else they could find to disagree about. They were all trying to be the biggest fish, all trying to reel someone in, all looking for the weakest swimmer in deep water. However, the fighters were just hungry and that was a good thing, because that meant they'd made the necessary sacrifices in preparation for the matches ahead. The boxers were called one by one to be weighed. There was a feeling of calm, mixed with nervous tension. The television cameras tried to capture our reality but the true reality was irrelevant. The greater picture is never revealed; though the cameras probe our faces for thought it remains unseen. I waited patiently. Then at last I was called to be weighed. I got on the scales and my weight was announced: 230 lb. Then my opponent took to the scales: 220 lb. In the heavyweight division anyone over 215 is a big and dangerous opponent. Tomorrow we would fight.

The night before a match never brings much, except waiting, sitting around and talking about other fighters. 'Maybe so-and-so can beat so-and-so or maybe not.' It was time to eat but someone had just failed to make the weight. It was a young kid from Mexico, the land of hard men. He spoke absolutely no English or German. Promoters were running around trying to find someone who spoke Spanish. They never looked twice at the fighters, much less at me. I approached them, asked what the problem was and said that I'd learnt some Spanish while travelling around Spain. They told me to tell him that he had an hour to make the weight or the fight was off.

I walked over and introduced myself, '*Hola, me llamo Mike. Los jeffes dijeron que tiennes una hora para complir el peso necesario. Si no puedes, tanto peor, buena suerte.*' He cursed their mothers, picked up his bag and left. His anger was understandable. Failure to make the correct weight can result in fines, cancelled bouts or both.

The odds were already up for the fights. There is no deceiving the bookmakers. They see and understand the odds from a distance. There's no relying on a hunch. A bookmaker looking into a horse's form, or a fighter's record, will see the years, the wins and the losses. Informed and knowledgeable, he sets the odds. So what of it? We still bet in company, in solitude, screaming for the winners we need to fulfil our goals.

Every fighter seems a kid, like me, holding onto his childhood like a favourite toy, clutching something furious in his blind fists, something like an Action Man. In the midnight hour I stood in front of the mirror with sleepless eyes and saw through my disguise. Was that really me? I feigned a look of surprise seeing myself quite clearly in the role I would be playing in the waiting ring. I had read the script and rehearsed unprompted: 'I must remember a tight defence. No butterflies. It's not sparring any more.' I'm on. I go through the dressing-room door into the arena to a tumultuous roar in my imagination. Clear as day in that mirror I felt almost physically my left and right hands absorbed in their shining illusion. Time magically in order, I had seen myself before in that reflection and at that point the night dissolved into a dreamy sleep. Its impression slid over me, though it remained vivid.

In the morning I woke with an inexplicable sense of relief that it was all over and that I had faced the battle with fear but also with joy and hope. Danger was waiting again. It could only be faced by men of war. I got up, took a shower and went down to the restaurant for breakfast with managers, promoters, fight fans, friends of fighters, hotel guests, all types of people. I knew the art that only seasoned professionals knew, which is to pass from one moment to the next and yet remain entirely in each one. The day of a fight is a day of meditation. God alone knows the colour that fate has in store for a man beyond the night. I blotted out my surroundings with a tape of NWA, Ice Cube and Dr Dre in my Walkman. Hip Hop for breakfast, dinner and tea. No love songs or mellow music to soften the mood while we waited for the coach to transfer human meat to the stadium where business is conducted with hands. Finally the time had arrived and there was no turning back.

I passed before the awesome Olympic stadium in Munich and thought, 'Wow!' Seeing its huge outline made me realise that at that minute sand would begin falling and would loosen to fill the glass of its universe. The sand had not yet reached that point where its descent starts to reflect our own sense of urgency. The fighters were escorted from the coach and into the stadium where the noise was deafening. I raised my head and saw tens of thousands of eyes positioned at angles so that every one could view the battleground. The small ring in the centre of the arena, like a new heart, was ready to supply the night with its rhythm. I looked into the ring where time would have its conquest and men their defeats. I recalled again the taste of this moment which happens before all fights, and how much I loved it. The rest of it didn't matter, not the trainers, managers or the promoters and their infighting. Not the boxing board and their demands, nor the probing cameras and reporters and certainly not the pain, though I accepted the pain. For me there's no escaping from the lust for experience. Who hasn't wanted to lay his life on the line, or stick his neck out without fear, scream with pain, cry, feel joy, grieve, love? All that is living. I made my way to the dressing rooms.

Finally the stadium was packed and the show could begin. For hours the first fighter had paced anxiously, dreaming of winning or losing but every show saw him draw first blood, usually at the speed of light. He would go about the task with a mind clouded in doubt. Nervously he would circle an opponent before opening their skull and smothering their face in blood. His hair was always combed and he would always leave the ring without a strand out of place. There seemed to be a silent misery in his black sunken eyes but silent men leave the loudest gift of pain.

The press flocked to him. They seemed to like his quiet language, spoken with ten fingers. He smiled with pleasure when they showed him the playback of the knockout in slow motion. 'The ultimate KO,' they called it. He felt a rush of blood through his body, a burst of energy as he relived the moment. Then he was released by the reporters to face life. There was no amount of knockouts that could fix his helplessness, self-doubt, social inadequacy or the transparent terror that being a fighter disguised.

The next fight saw arms raised high into the night as the kid from Mexico brought his gloves to his chin and dropped his hands. Just like that, he was unconscious covering the canvas, stretched out on his back. Maybe the struggle to make the weight had affected him. Back in the dressing room the poor boy waited for courage. The bravery to talk to his trainer, who was also his father, and look him in his eyes. Later I saw a father hug his son like a grown man who'd just learnt a valuable lesson.

Then I heard him say in Spanish to his son, 'Life moves forward and what's done can't be undone. Time won't move in the opposite direction, so raise your head. You lost a fight, that's all. Everyone loses in life. A man takes what life offers him on the chin and gets up in order to stay alive without excuse or self-pity and fights on without comment.'

He felt humiliated. It was his first loss. The problem was that the boy knew they'd pass judgement, looking down on him not so silently from comfortable armchairs in front of TV screens. As a boxer I don't think people who pass judgement can live without the things they judge. Why can't they find something else to do where they can become the main characters? Though I do sympathise with their armchair existence. Some people are born with talent, some are not.

Finally it was time to start putting on the armour that transforms actual men into boxers. I often lose myself in the process. It's at that point that all things leave me, all but one, the fight. The first thing I do is set everything out on a chair in the right order and then get undressed to my underpants. I then proceed in a definite order. Nothing is left to mere chance. I put on my socks, always left to right. Then my boots, lacing them up left to right. Third, the binding of hands. There's always a certain pleasure watching Bob Shannon tape hands. He's a painter and decorator by trade and brings the same level of perfection and professionalism to the job. Taping is the most important thing for me because I'll need my hands for my next life, the life of a bassist. He also tapes left to right.

Then on goes the groin guard and shorts. Oiling down comes next. First my legs, left to right, then arms left to right, followed by my back and chest. Vaseline is then applied to the eyebrows and cheeks, then the gumshield is washed and kept by the trainer until I enter the ring. The last thing is the gloving-up of the fighter, always left to right. Anticipation ran through my body. The sweat began a slow trickle upon my brow. I walked round and round, paced the floor and thought, 'Not too long now.'

You might laugh at the methodical preparation being performed from left to right. Superstition is a question unanswered, an answer unknown. A thing that grows with time, passed down hand to hand through generations. It is a thing we easily believe and sometimes we are blinded by its faith. I understand it to be a way of hiding from reality but its reassurance makes me feel safe.

I took my time but still I had to wait to be gloved-up, searching for my shadow among the stars. At last my hour had come. Officials shot past with urgent errands. We stood eager, cool and ready. For a month we'd trained happily in our respective gyms. Now the air was hostile with bright lights peering into our souls, searching for nerves or fear. Tonight the opponent is seen. The fight is real. We knew these tedious past weeks had been a prelude to a tear-up. The realisation resurrected our fears. We had waited for this. Our thoughts began a voyage through dreams, hopes and the routine of a fighter's life while we waited silently. I had been preparing in my dressing room most of the night, visualising his hands, the sweating detachment of limbs and the victory I owned.

I've been here before on the stage, calculating swift tactics while waiting for my moment to wage war. Waiting to hear them call out my name, knowing that the battle had to be fought. How natural is that state? Though I was quite sure for what prize I fought I was unable to think beyond the night. Amidst my many thoughts was the awareness that my opponent was somebody's son: proud of his skills; strong in flesh and bone; steel in his chin; borne on with desire to knock me out.

THE JOURNEYMAN

Every time I cross from this prearranged world into a ring where anything can happen, a place alone, different and detached from this reality, I ask 'Why?' I have embraced the ring with pleasure, never worrying if my blood would be sufficient to support my family's thirst. Pain was the measure of my dedication. Last month I hurt a man, soon I shall hurt another, or be hurt myself and we shall be satisfied to be applauded for causing the other's pain. Soon I will arrive into the roar of screaming fans. I won't be late to face the fury in my opponent's fists. The flames of adrenaline have begun to burn in my stomach. Humanity's mortal fears have begun to invade my body. All of which tells me I'm ready. I breathed in deeply the air, charged with things to come, as the unknown prepared its invasion.

Standing in front of the mirror before the long walk to the ring, I chose silence. I looked at my hands bound with blank tape and squeezed into ten ounces of leather ready to fly like angels, all dazzling speed and brutality. My opponents were at home with these fists. They were strong enough to be gentle, but these hungry hands would tear everything down. They could even break bread angrily. These gentle imprisoned terrors, bound in leather, would drop strangers from enormous heights. Darkness tears down the light and agony begins there. Dream by dream, the timekeeper counted his victim. Interesting patterns of blood on the floor brought into focus the mortal realisation that hands tell the time. Roaring crimson fell from huge bodies and covered the canvas like a quilt, bringing urgent doctors to work.

The ring is infected by weightless dreams, unanchored hopes, and inhabited by men for whom there is another truth. Yet I know men who are most alive in its centre. Men who leave their private pain behind, out of mind, to fight against gravity's inevitable pull. Here men's dreams can be interrupted by dark horizons and suspended on light blue canvas under artificial light. Here slow counts are mumbled between illuminated lips, again perceptible through declining shadows. I dreamt that the brave might rise from battle before ten disenchanted seconds and snatch victory from another mouth of broken teeth. The brave did rise before me but as the night unfolded they vanished before my eyes. Only their bloodstains remained.

From this roped space we watch and are observed in our pain. Here is the destination of a warrior's resurrected spirit. Here is where we forget the numb bewilderment of our true realities. Here the bonding of man's soul is strong. Here a pawn on a boxing chessboard can achieve his dream and become a queen. When an opponent stands in front of me I know his intention well enough not to try reasoning. Hands have the answer to all the problems in our lives. Hands care nothing for thought with no margin for error. There's something dangerous in ten hungry fingers that move faster than their shadow. My mind must be constantly aware of them.

It was my time but before I could cross the ropes I had the long walk, the ring walk. I moved slowly. My mind was empty of all things except my opponent. My throat was dry. The air was heavy like a leaden weight and a million crazed eyes full of curiosity watched me taking small steps. What a feeling of liberation I felt as I walked out into their applause. The under card had served to whet their appetite. Designer aftershave filled the air. The ring card girls kept the audience keen. I was torn between the sound of the crowd and my own deafening silence, both distorted almost beyond recognition. But I was there to break their sound. I wanted to silence the German fans as I had done once before some years earlier in Hamburg. On that occasion I had been brought over from England on short notice to be beaten up and sent home.

Barry McGuigan very kindly entered my dressing room and proceeded to advise me on how to fight the German, Markus Bott. My attention was captured by his melodic Irish accent. Having never before seen or heard of Bott, I listened gratefully.

Annihilation was a thing most foreign to the Germans, whose matchmakers are among the most careful in the world. Markus Bott had become such a nuisance until two hands arrived in round seven. They called themselves K and O. They arrived just as energy was fading. They unloaded all that they had to put him down and out for the count. His soul returned to his aching body and forced his bleeding eyes to open in spite of the invading light. He came round in his corner, finding himself propped up on a stool, painfully aware that he'd underestimated me. That was a night the Germans and their press have never forgotten. Now I was a recognised boxer in Germany who signed autographs for their fans.

My senses seemed more than a dream. I was here again in the flesh and ready to play my part. I walked on. I was to enter the ring first and make my way to the red corner. I began to hear the music I had requested through the overwhelming frequencies of the night. The strong beats of Hip Hop. Its rhythms helped me to compress the moment. I lingered and loitered, slowed down my walk, floated in oblivion, relaxed in the pleasure of the moment. I bathed in the glory of it, breathed in the present and exhaled all doubt. Finally I arrived at the ring which stood like a stage awaiting the actors. I climbed the steps, walked to the red corner and stood waiting, half-naked. Next, my opponent entered the ring. He cut a large solitary figure that stood apart from the people around him staring into the night, blinded by his heart's vision of his dreams. Could the night deliver what the day had promised him?

One by one the ring emptied. The fight must go on, the body's routine, the usual work, a return to pain. Time had arrived with encouraging words. The referee commanded the fighters to turn towards each other and meet with hungry eyes. Time to measure the other's fear. We wanted to establish our silent attitudes and define the qualities behind our struggle. His eyes were full of a furious urge, armed indifference, and held a sense of oblivion. The referee checked that our groinguards and gumshields were in place and mumbled the rules over the noise in the stadium. He still burned with the sacrifice of an old fighter and remained dedicated to what was normal in his life. Tenacity still survives in a body sustained by air and dreams. He ordered fretful hands to touch gloves. I held out my left arm. Imaginary shadows met in a dance for life. A physical discussion would dispel the dreams of a boy.

Last-minute advice came flooding in. 'Be positive. You can win this. It doesn't matter how big he is. As soon as the bell rings, go forward. Don't forget to use the jab. Don't move in straight lines, make angles. Move side to side. Keep your hands high. Throw combinations. Watch out for his left hook. Start fast but take your time. Preserve energy. Relax. Forget the cameras. Do it for your kids! It's just you and him. Plenty of movement. On your toes. In and out. Bend your legs. Bob and weave. Rough him up. Plenty of body shots. No head-hunting. Good boxing. Do whatever you have to do to win. It's up to you. Good luck!'

17

THE FIGHT

Round one. A thoughtful start with defence well prepared. Mavrovic dipped and bounced in the opening minute, looking for an opportunity to attack, his right hand cocked and ready to punish a slow left by throwing the right over the top of it. He stayed up on his toes, firing the occasional jab which I slipped and rolled under. I knew he was looking to find his range. He was trying to dictate how the fight should be. I wanted to stem the flow of adrenaline bubbling through his veins. I upped the pace and opened up on his mid-section with a painful, rib-roasting flurry. Then a quick left-right jarred me and I retreated across the ring and got crafty. But nothing confused him, neither pain nor kidology spoiled his certainty. He was aggressive. I went to the body to slow him down. I had the impression that sustained pressure might get the job done early. A dirty right to my kidneys escaped the referee's attention. I looked at my opponent. What was to be learnt was not in a manual, but in taking your body through an hour against itself. So the fight began. Only one would conquer that hour. There was only room for one hero and a life's ambition was within both our horizons. It didn't matter what you'd done before, who you'd fought or where you'd been.

A minute's rest. All that was swift sat motionless, guard down. Certain of no definition, we were linked to one another. Assembled under naked lights to contemplate the recurring mystery that competition forces on us. Bob whispered, 'Have a drink, spit into the bucket, don't drink too much water. Remember the plan, come back to it. Don't fight his fight, you need to get close and cut down the distance and don't stand still in front of him. Use your jab. Don't load up, he can see your right hand cocked and waiting. Don't be so rigid. Get back out there and win. Relax, breathe, you won that round.'

Round two. He was strong and exuded energy. I waited for him to make a mistake that I could capitalise on. His hands felt heavier, with more weight behind them, like he was armed with blackjacks or cleavers or brass knuckles. I started to obey their repetitive insistence. I responded by forcing myself into the uncomfortable role of hunter and followed with a handful of jabs before bludgeoning him with a left to the forehead and an overhand right. Boom! The combination was a perfect illustration of wasted talent and potential. Not only were the punches delivered with frightening speed but the second punch was thrown at a different angle than he expected. He came back with a left-right combination but minimised their effect by jumping in. Thus began a series of brilliant exchanges that continued for the remainder of the round. His confidence began to grow, supported by amazing roars from a section of the crowd that sometimes echoed the sound of crashing. Jarring hands launched at me, ricocheting off my head and gloves. I realised the power he had in both hands. Unseen and abstract dangers came into sight. But your heart wins from confronting life. I spent the round's last minute behind a high guard.

A minute's rest. I sat surrounded by the minute filled with the sound of Bob's voice. I felt his fingers massaging the areas where rage had congested and lactic acid was beginning to flood. Surrounded by the silence a boxer feels in the ring, my mind wandered. The champion who shadowboxed inside my head thought I could win if

I could hold out against his excessive passion and evident courage. Bob told me to keep cool and not to get involved. He said, 'Concentrate, realise that what seems like nothing is really quite a lot. The openings are everywhere. Use your experience.'

He was telling me to use the inherent abilities simmering below the surface waiting to be allowed out, set free by the only one who could . . . me. The laws of tension, pre-calculation, reason, aggression and intrigue are all part of the game. Then he spread Vaseline on my brow, gave me water and replaced my gumshield, removed my stool and climbed down. My opponent took advice from his corner while standing, waiting for the bell.

Round three. As I came out for work my chest rose and fell. Powerful beats accelerated, my body contemplated movement and my respiratory apparatus drew in strong breaths. Sweat ran down the bridge of my nose like a leaking faucet. I hardly had the time to think about what I was going to do. He made his intentions clear and came steaming towards me in a hot rush of adrenaline. My jab worked well. I turned my shoulders and caught his punches. I had to think about conservation of energy for the later rounds whilst balancing a fragmented future on my shoulders. His hands were brilliant, insistent, fast and heavy. The crowd were enjoying it. They chanted his name and roared with approval every time he launched his punches. My lungs began to feel the tug of time. I began pacing my attacks. I followed a flurry of activity with circular movements, keeping my advancing opponent at bay with a solid left jab. His arrogant smile urged me towards confrontation. There was no scriptwriter here. No expert to choreograph the violence. The referee was not a director who could shout 'Cut!' if things went wrong. In the third minute of the round he flaunted his speed by releasing a multi-punch barrage. Only one or two of the blows found their intended target. He was throwing every blow with the intention of doing as much damage as was possible to break down my resistance. I wanted to rest my arms. Then I heard my corner shouting and got my hands up. I saw my opponent drop his guard and fired a right hand that hurt him. He put them up again. I went back downstairs beneath his ribcage and saw he was worried. He jerked my head to the side with a left hook. I responded with a right hand. Keeping my hands high I fell exhausted against the ropes and fired wildly towards him.

A minute's rest. 'This is it, Mike, what the fuck are you waiting for?' The voice in my corner rose. 'Listen to what I'm telling you. This is your life so get out there and live it.'

'I'm trying to.'

'What's the matter with you?' Bob said. 'Move your head from side to side.'

Then I felt a palmed hand across my face followed by a shout that was repeated over and over. 'How much do you want it? How much do you want it? You can be tired the rest of your life.'

I knew what he meant. When fighting, boxers can know nothing of rest. That's the single fact we acknowledge of ourselves. Our personal identities recede into pure recollection much like an illusion which only expendable flesh makes real. The seconds that people themselves in a shapeless minute reshaped into a desire to win. Only the fittest survive the outpouring of pain without resolution, without love or trust. The crowd, on the other hand, applauded any acceptable beating like trained seals. Time was sucking the air from my lungs. Administered blows were accumulating and promising to crack open my wig. At this rate my battered brain would remember nothing. That would appeal to the promoter. A surer ground for his own takings, another night's hustle completed. There is a certain economic freedom bought with blood and time. It's just a natural thing.

Round four. I took a moment to consider the fact that our brutality would prove itself profitable. Mavrovic was intelligent and fought hard for his kids and their mother. He found me smooth and slippery and was almost buried when my hands found their opportunity. I too had children and a wife whose lives I fought hard for. My heart knew the moment when it has to answer that all-important question. 'How much do you really want this?'

I fought on to define an undefined destiny. But tiredness was forcing me to look past my opponent's image into the face of the timekeeper. I faked to the body and fired a lead right to his head. His eye immediately swelled almost shut. I forced him into the corner and smashed a right uppercut to his gloves, then another. He grabbed me around the neck and pushed my head down, crudely trying to rough me up. He knew the art of tying up a fighter. The referee broke the clinch. He spent the remainder of the round running, slipping and holding. I tried to walk him down, hoping to get close enough to land a good right but became frustrated. I just couldn't get it off.

Another rest. I had responded to my opponent's attacks through the aching pain of successive human minutes and I knew that despite fatigue I would again have to advance. Wishful dreams began to disappear in the flow of water from a wet sponge over my head. The seconds grew, stretching without pause. The referee came to my corner during the rest period and ordered the mopping up of excessive fluid around my stool. I tried to keep the faith and waited for the next bell to move me. I dragged meditating hands to their feet.

Round five. The music moved into double time and the heart asked questions about time signature. We exchanged bone-crunching combinations but my opponent's punches always felt that bit sharper. I buckled his legs for a moment with a left hook and forced him back to the ropes but he rallied fiercely, letting both hands fly left and right that turned into hooks and uppercuts. When I hurt him he got stronger and looked more destructive. I gave everything to take his heart but still I was sliding towards defeat. Then, without first giving me a warning, the referee deducted a point for a low blow. It was turning into a long and wearying fight, but I wasn't going to sit back and quit. Nor would I start exhausting myself with futile efforts to box too hard. I just gave myself a forward push and again I tried to step up the tempo, pumping out resilience and hope. For a brief moment I saw the fear of a child drop from his eyes. I struck swift and sure with dogged determination. We were just two boys doing what we had to in order to survive.

A minute's rest. I returned to stillness after a harassing three minutes of thunderous exchanges. Then I spat their boiling memories into a bucket held out for me after gargling with their bitter taste. Whispered words brought my blood to a slow boil until my veins began to overflow with enthusiastic energy. My rested heart's circulation grew stronger. I could feel its rhythm. I rose for the next round with eight ounces of dynamite strapped to each hand. The next three minutes would explode into the memory of all who witnessed its brutality.

Round six. For me a tough fight was predicted, but not for him. I made my body respond to my renewed enthusiasm for the fight, forcing it to realise my ambition. Neither one of us took a backward step for a minute and a half. Within our embattled space we exchanged heavy punches in barrages to both body and head, until I couldn't breathe and backed off to catch my breath, keeping my gloves by my head and elbows tucked into my ribs, knowing he would come again. I heard Bob shouting from the corner, 'Use the jab!' I parried and blocked his punches then held out my arm in his face to keep him off. Through pain and gloved hunger grew the strength, though fragile, of an animal conscious of his desires. The flesh that rose and fell stood in centre ring ready to taste the sweetness of victory or the agony of defeat.

Dry tongues remember their hatred of thirst. Each gloved hand is a slave that in turn enslaves the other. We played together with darkness. Fighting against shadows of tired flesh flooded with lactic acid. We were conscious of the muscular bodies we dragged into the ring of reality. Escaping thought, a man becomes entirely body in the moment when gloves touch under instruction: eager for the slaughter of light in the confrontations of darkness on a blue canvas floor.

THE JOURNEYMAN

I knew that later I would feel a strange gratitude when I went home to my family and felt their tender kisses on my wounds. I would forget the pain, the fatigue, the rage of thunder hands. When I'm home with the love that makes everything worthwhile, hunger will be satisfied in that moment. But now he was circling, growing in confidence. His fast combinations were stealing rounds from me, though I felt that as long as he remained on his feet the German referee guaranteed them to him.

A minute's rest. The round and thoughts recycled themselves. The most extensive struggle was found in the inner space where the mind waited the return of its motivation. My inner voice screamed out loud. 'Get off this stool and be saluted, battered body, towering spirit. Rise in spite of the savaging perpetrated on you. Your courage must be greater.'

A thin ribbon of blood trickled down from my nose. 'Yes, taste your own mortal blood and get off this stool in spite of your pain and claim your victory.'

In the beginning lashes were given to unruly men thrown into pairs, branded with hot irons and ordered to drown in their own blood. Brutal spectacles of developed hands, stiffened by rigid coils entwined with lead and iron, wouldn't be enough for the bloodthirsty spectator. Spikes replaced lead and iron to ensure a certain death on the yellow sands of Greek and Roman arenas, where the audience decided whether to spare the life of a fallen warrior or let him die, with a simple gesture of thumbs.

All eyes were on those who took the heads of lions. The public saw how the fighters suffered and knew they needed rest. Stadiums stared wide-eyed then slipped away with quenched thirst. How many died in those far-away arenas of the world? Their hopes taken at the shoulders, heads littering the earth and hands reaching out for swords, to die with gladiator's pride. Their bodies were stacked like timber and awaited the flame that set souls free. I could have been there with them, but instead I am here, a poor man fighting for small salaries in the last permitted place for a true warrior: the boxing ring.

Some of us still live to fight and indulge in gladiatorial dreams. We rise and run at dawn in search of wealth, unafraid with no illusions of safety. Were we meant to survive in this civilised world? We're not supposed to be doing this out of love. But who understands the inbuilt rage inherited from the blood of slaves with roaring spirits and restless souls in search of respect? The ghosts of dead warriors fill our inner worlds with their spiked fists, naked fists, gloved fists and lean bodies caked in drying blood. They embrace the realities of burning hunger, standing face to face with the image of itself. I stared across the ring at the end of the minute to where my opponent turned his head and our eyes met. The vision meant nothing to us because we now lived under the shadows of confronting desires and it's not a world easily understood.

Round seven. He rose and walked towards me. I held the centre. His eyes caught mine. I threw an urgent punch with intent. There was nothing else, no wrist, no arm, just a fist. He swerved away. Was he becoming weaker or stronger? I wasn't sure. A fighter's knowledge was trickling through my fingers. One hand carried defeat like a bomb under a coat, the other held the past, present and future. An argument erupted between the mind and the body. It felt like my mind was urging my body on, full of hope that I could win. But my body felt the rounds counting themselves, minute by minute, the seconds hammering it. It was tired of the numbers, tired under the lights in that heated stadium.

I wanted release from the body's treacheries, to be engaged by something else, like desire and passion or at least by the anger that lurked behind my dreams. My feet moved on knowing that under them the ground was still firm. My arms extended, muscle defined, in independent flight. We became entangled and eyes stared over the other's shoulders towards a life where food stretches and new cars overflow from garages attached to silent houses where privileges are forgotten.

A minute's rest. I fought with it breathlessly. My shoulders were tired. I had felt him searching for my rhythm, or the timing of my rhythm. His eyes traced my footsteps on the canvas but instead I found my way inside his beat where the heart's calculated thoughts overflow. I couldn't let time have its way. Winners somehow trust what comes before the mind's eye (or the heart's eye) and are compelled to give their all. Down the road they came, old memories stumbling with torn flesh on broken knuckles. I waited in the silent centre of brutal time. The sweetness of our dreams are bloodied by wounded hands as they advance through a harsh world of men whose hearts grow more tired every round. Knowing the recipe of what it takes to make a champion, I brought negative images of self to boil in their memory of youth. I added a touch of pain to the rage that stifles itself. I mixed a spoon of pride with the blood of a dead father over a minute's fire and watched energy burst until I was ready to explode. Bob, point me in the right direction. I could still feel a gladiator's pride accumulating over the fire, assured and insistent upon my duty. I felt a change, a unique moment. I was becoming a different man than the man before that minute. Sixty seconds later and the sound of the bell was lost in the roar of the crowd. It was all or nothing and I knew nothing else. A runner clocks the miles and collects the sponsorships. Born with a gift for words, one writes a sentence and makes it pay. A singer sings. A soldier fights wars.

Round eight. This guy was giving me nothing but trouble, the left jab, the angles he threw them at. I'm saying it hurt to walk onto them. Mainly it was the right hand I worried about. The right cross they call it: very dangerous. There's no fun in going headfirst into one, or a hook, uppercut or overhand right for that matter. They're all one and the same connecting on your chin. He looks pumped and ready to deliver a whole bunch of fists, but what the hell. What state of mind is it when nothing matters any more? Were those really my thoughts? He was tough and moved with ease, forcing me to stumble into combinations of counter-punches. He was used to finishing guys when he hurt them and exploded with a blitz. My lack of conditioning made me clumsy. Head down, I charged like a bull.

It felt like a dream I'd had; me attacking a phantom cape put in front of me by a faceless matador. I would go forward but he dodged every time and the crowd roared with laughter. I tried again and another roar filled the stands. I had no hope of catching him or defending my over-nourished body against his sword or the picador's spears.

Had I forgotten my life and what it's like to fight for survival? Always last in line. First come, first served. I had to remember that. If I passed through the pain maybe I could start over and be respected. I went back behind the jab and threw methodical combinations but there was something chilling in my opponent's ambition. He didn't just want to win. He wanted to break my heart. Then a right cross and a left hook to my head and suddenly, for what seemed like the longest time, I lay in an abyss of dark light that cast shadowy patterns on my battered face and tired arms. I stared upwards unseeing with large-pupilled eyes gazing into the blackness that had fallen on me and fought against the desire to become one with dark sleep. The broken rhythm of fists in flight brought this black slumber back into focus. With time came a relentless funeral beat that slowly moved blood through thirsty vessels until light broke through and flooded an empty mind with conscious thought. Seven . . . Eight . . . Get up! 'What am I doing down here?' A boisterous heart beat life back into stiffened limbs and I rose at the count of nine. The referee motioned me to walk towards him. Mavrovic had climbed the ring-post in premature celebration. He thought it was over. The referee let the fight continue but seemed to be hovering a bit closer to the activity just in case his intervention was necessary. It wasn't. I came through it.

A minute's rest. 'Come on!' Bob exhorted as he took the gumshield from my mouth. 'It's not over yet, come on!' Then he went to work on a small cut that had opened over my left eye just under my eyebrow. He battled to staunch the blood, covering me in Vaseline, but the referee ordered it removed. I was losing my face. My handsome features no longer existed. The possible and the impossible were now the same, merging into the impulse of man and beast somersaulting around one another, both panting dog-like in confrontation, vain and unseeing. Forget about the cut. This is boxing. You bleed. I was still a little dazed from the heat of hands that tried to set fire to my courage. Blood ran from my face. I was running out of time. The hourglass was draining of vital grains. Once again I waited for the bell.

Round nine. Predator and prey circled each other covered in blood. Steam rose from our shoulders. We shifted from one leg to another, listening to each other's breathing with hands held high through a hard round. Enormous hearts unrivalled, burning souls permanent, expanded lungs puffed like toads on air-conditioned rocks. The ambitious eyes of physical forms dazzle through moments of nervous energy. Battered bodies, no rest, explosive hands watching the clock, waiting, wondering 'How long can three minutes be?' I was exhausted. My poor heart was being tossed about. My opponent was still strong. He was a fitness fanatic who had prepared for this fight by going into training camp for weeks before the fight because he had the money to get away from family life and other distractions. He was the Heavyweight Champion of Europe, which meant that he could afford a team consisting of conditioners and nutritionists as well as trainers with different skills. Although I'd been in Denmark, I was still a late substitute lacking the time to become a 100 per cent fit.

Do you understand the struggle? It doesn't matter if you don't understand our lives and how our characters are shaped by the need to fight. Life on the streets isn't easy to understand but the struggle to eat is easily comprehended. It's not difficult to be reasonable. We accept our situations and know how far we can go. Our survival really does come down to the fittest, strongest and most cunning. We do have to face the man in the mirror and ask questions about our hearts before we truly know that we belong to this moment. We build the strength to take possession of defeat and victory equally, without hiding from the consequences. I am labelled a journeyman.

I find myself involved in ring wars with champions, without proper preparation. How can anyone expect an unfit body to be the champion I know myself to be? For a fighting man this is frustrating. Everything I told my hands was interrupted by fitter, faster fists that dropped like grenades around my head. How could I make my work count or take a bearing on my opponent's head whilst hiding between my gloves? Maybe the chance to check his heart foolishly rushing in would present itself, though now I was armed only with desire, wishing I could go back to the gym to prepare again for this moment. Work out daily with extra miles on the road, again to unfold in this centre as the champion I know myself to be.

A minute's rest. He sat on his stool with half-closed eyes. What words did his corner whisper away from invading microphones in a stadium of ears? He looked over his shoulders but I knew from experience how hard it is to distinguish anything in those times when a minute gets shorter with every breath. Fatigue brings thoughts in fragments and allows fury to fade. Time amplifies moments and controls judgement. Danger advances in millimetres and the prey prepares his defence against a fierce predator. But who's sure who is prey and who is predator? Once more I rose. The fatigue almost made the round's journey too difficult to begin again. My lungs fought for breathing space. A brave heart demonstrated its courage by lifting damaged flesh in search of victory: to continue stumbling into pain and dark shadows. Fury increased but who would deal with the broken body and make way for a champion?

Round ten. I fought alone with a pounding chest. The shadows came close then were far apart. The bloodthirsty crowd was eager for its spill, ready to witness the mingling of red splatter. By now we both must have been fighting back our tears in pursuit of glory, holding onto our injuries round after round. I unloaded my weapons, a right hand uppercut which sent a ripple through his legs. He touched down for a brief count. A brave man commands the respect of the world. All eyes were on him as he rose. Compassion still existed in my severed heart. Its humanity remained intact.

A minute's rest. Someone would be beaten in the next rounds. The final two rounds. Fists had begun to bleed and for one of us the pain would take over. I looked across the ring as far as I could with a naked eye and all I could see were the tracks of blood where tough kids played. We spent the entire minute looking into the faces of our trainers who did everything they could to help us find a place for ourselves in our minds. I had planned to get to the end of the fight as quickly as possible. We don't get paid for overtime, it was just a matter of cutting this man down and planting him somewhere else. Had I prepared, I could have achieved my goal. I saw him read my thoughts, write his ending to tonight's script and prepare to take victory for himself.

Round eleven. The round was in the balance until the position and severity of the cut forced the referee to lead me to the ringside physician. He inspected the damage and, remarkably, allowed me to continue. Suddenly the cut re-opened over one eye then the other. Falling like a great waterfall, blinding blood flooded both eye sockets. Red-faced, swollen head growing, pulsating temples sped their rhythm. My wounds were getting worse. I was amazed that I'd risen in the earlier rounds. I was unable to see my opponent's combinations. Darkness awaited. Only seconds of conscious time left, seconds that seemed like minutes, hours. A blackbird dressed in a white bloodstained shirt and black bow tie flew in circles around the perimeter of the nightmare. The sound of the eleventh bell ended the ordeal and the buzzing flies swarmed. The blood spill brought the bout to a premature end. It had to go to the score cards for a technical decision. The Croatian immediately raised his arms. The crowd stood and applauded.

Minutes, seconds burnt in memory that never passed. I leaned upon the perimeter of a dream we'd just shared, back pressed against the ropes that contained our fury, watched by examining eyes that craved only blood. For many weeks our tired bodies ran down empty streets and tortured themselves through hours of gym work, developing habits that led us to this night. One winner, one loser: two broken, half-naked men kept from sleep by conditioning. Friends that respected each other embraced, wounds still bleeding.

Weapons rested, the referee crossed the canvas and collected the scorecards. What price paid our salaries? What a fight! For an hour life imparted its lessons. We were merciless in pursuit of each other's head and deserved the other's appreciation. We'd trained day and night for a win, made our bodies strong with pain. We knocked each other down and pride's whip made us rise from the dust. Dedication was not enough to stop gloved daggers but we continued, ignoring the dazzling lights and the animated crowd. Quietening our fears with confidence and inspired courage, we demonstrated all that we had so painfully learnt. Everyone congratulated us. We thanked each other for a great fight and our emotions where such that we embraced again.

Blood brought a premature end to the night. I didn't see round twelve. Without fear I had thrown myself in the direction of intimacy though its barrels were pointing toward me. In my hunger I found meagre crumbs of affection. Our silent fury was watched by our body's masters. They watched us savage the hearts they fed to us while conspiring with mountains of twisted organisms to spoil our moment by feeding us our own beating organs. How could I accept my own need for water? Centuries of sun had dried my body of precious sweat but I loved the heat and confronting my thirst, now intensified by eleven hard rounds of boxing, would've broken her heart. My bitter soul complained to the heavens but the gods hadn't harmed me. The desire to win had turned against me, struck and beaten me to its will. A dream is a quiet man whose eyes are hardened to tears and whose soul will rise again from gravity's pull. To take what he needs from life, to stop time at his will.

18

THE WILL TO LIFE

I rose from defeat, beaten and unsatisfied. I walked among the animated crowd, skin covered in sweat and blood. They were appreciative of my effort. Some even bent over railings as I passed and tapped me on the back. I heard the sound of applause and my name on their tongues thrilled me. The sounds were sounds of victory and I was victory's slave. I gave my autograph to anyone who would have one. Was it possible I could be a winner and after tonight some would recognise me as more than just a journeyman? While I contemplated my position the cameras passed me by and journalists interviewed the other guy; the one I wanted to knock out but couldn't. Do reporters know what it's like to almost be somebody, left behind to roam in self-doubt with one thought? How do I extinguish thought? I accepted my defeat and shook the hand that wounded me. No matter how many times he knocked me down I got up, my mouth overflowing with blood. The chewed gumshield was evidence of a savage 11 rounds. I recalled the road I had travelled to this battle, how little work I'd put into my preparation and how much I had stopped to rest. I had already sharpened my hands and mastered their skill but they were useless against his strength. I stood fierce in the middle of nowhere, disheartened.

THE JOURNEYMAN

Once again I came away with nothing. Luck had again abandoned me and left me unfit in a hostile climate. But part of me believed, and still believes, that I could cast off the negative feelings of loss and be the champion too.

I went into this fight with no fear of the fists that ripped through my flesh, because it wasn't the first time I'd been beaten. We all lose, fighting against relentless time and I'd sworn on my life, no more fear. I dragged my exhausted body back to the dressing room suffering noble wounds, my hopes weighted by kryptonite. I unwrapped my weapons and stood under a shower to wash away both the blood and its memory. But motionless memories held onto their pain. Tonight, as on some other occasions, I'd failed to impress myself. In other fights I'd possessed the enemy, eaten his will, taken his craft, but still I'd failed, betrayed then (as now) by my own body. However, the most unnameable desire to do it all again would return. Boxing is a drug so sweet that even children watch and smile. Broken bones, blackened eyes, all by themselves become a passion.

Henry Maska, a German Light-heavyweight and World Champion topped the bill on that Munich night and became a national hero. He made a fortune from the ring and was treated like a movie star in his own country.

Back at the hotel there was an after-fight party thrown by the sponsors Hallecoder, the German beer company. The thirsty hotel filled with celebrities, actors, sportsmen and women, fight fans and hangers-on. They all soaked up the free beer, ate all the free food then drank some more. Even those who didn't drink filled their glasses to overflowing. They drank and danced to their own music. They drank and revelled all the night. No one stayed sober. I piled up my plate with food then packed a bowl with trifle. Then I filled half a dozen glasses with beer. Tell me why everyone should be drinking and not me. I was tired, bruised, with a swollen head and stiff joints. I sated myself then decided to get some sleep. I had an early flight back to Manchester and the music was becoming too loud for me to hear myself think. I told Bob I'd see him in the morning and went up to my room.

I lay down, crumbling like bread onto the bed, settled in and watched television, flicking through endless channels until I found the porn that all the best German hotels provide. I watched for a while until I could think of nothing but the desire to penetrate. I fantasised about the first time I'd met Angela. I was trying to masturbate while it was still dark outside but I had the unmistakable feeling I was being watched. I got up and looked around. I checked the bathroom. Nothing, of course. I was taking no chances so I checked the door. It was locked. So I turned off the light and went back to bed. The feeling had passed and I drifted off into sleep.

I returned home looking forward to seeing Angela, her body still beautiful after three children. She stood in innocent silence waiting for the rain to stop. The only sound was the swishing of the water made by passing traffic. I shut the taxi door behind me and looked across the road at a vision of love that controlled my sight with no room for anything else. I crossed the road and pulled her close enough to see my reflection in her eyes and she saw hers in mine.

I had hoped that by some remote chance Jack Trickett could secure a rematch. It never happened. Soon after our bout my opponent relinquished the European Heavyweight title he had held to contest the world title belts held by our own Lennox Lewis. I saw a proud creature at his work again. He gave Lewis 12 hard rounds, taking everything Lewis had to offer, but was unsuccessful in his attempt. It was his desire that hurt him, not the fight, though I'd seen for myself and understood the innocence in his need. Not so immortal, I heard that a real war had begun and this time his opponent, hepatitis, set the rules. For him the fight we fought was just a dress rehearsal for the greater struggle that would take place within his own failing body. Zeljko Mavrovic, a German-based Croatian, was born to fight. A true fighter inspires others, blessed with talent and heart. Though great warriors have kindness in reserve, they are willing to wound and stand attentive to their applause. The vacant European Heavyweight title was picked up by Vitali Klitschko, a German-based Russian.

After I got back from Munich there was a spell of inactivity, a time I couldn't get a fight. No one was keen to meet me in the ring and matchmakers wouldn't take the chance. They wouldn't put their prospects into a 50/50 situation. I had to make a living. I began to teach high school students the bass and trumpet privately. Showing how the notes hummed within the music they made. How they bounce in rhythmic joy, join in wonderful melodies and how harmonies become a song. I taught them how to paint expressive colours for the ears to feel and how to allow the source to work through them. As a teacher I try to let confident voices emerge from their origin and mount the throats of the young to bring change from their depths. It was especially pleasing to teach others, knowing that my two boys Cassius and Clay had become fine trumpeters, playing in some of the best concert halls across the North-west with the Manchester Youth Brass Band. Can anything be more delightful than its inspiration? I love jazz and my beautiful Angela. Both make my blood run and skin tingle. I could sit and listen for hours or take all the time in the world to please Angela. I love these two things and everyday I give thanks for having them in my life.

A night caught me unaware. I had no idea it was coming. We'd all got a little drunk when Angela and I were having dinner at a friend's house. They were a young couple who had both got boozy and had let the food get cold. No one was hungry anyway.

'How much do fighters really get paid?' a curious woman asked me. She was sitting to my left. I didn't even know her name. She seemed like twelve people rolled into one, deciding my fate. I told her that it depended on who you fought.

She deliberated and responded with. 'I've never met a boxer before but it seems to me that if someone had gone to school and studied for a good career they wouldn't box.' She was without doubt. I felt like the accused. She continued, 'An intelligent man would never allow himself to be half-naked fighting like a beast in a boxing ring.'

I hated being cross-examined. The jurors sat around the dinner table listening carefully to what was being said. I prepared my defence, saying that I didn't think she understood and that it was hard to explain. I tried to illustrate my argument in terms of a Nietzschean will to power, that this was how I saw existence: a collection of great and small struggles revolving round superiority, growth and expansion; that these power struggles were governed in accordance with the selfsame will to power, a will to life. I followed this with my love for the game and asked for her response, hoping this informal dinner-table jury could judge me fairly.

She turned to stone and said. 'I don't like fighting. I don't like fighters and I don't know why the hell I wasted my time talking to you!'

I've run into comments like this before, and will do again. The boxing ring tells people nothing of the mind. Negative stereotypes are its history; fighters with blunted nerves who left no recorded message, who fell unnamed on bloody canvas floors. As a boxer, it is too easy to be labelled violent, uncounted, unseen; the world doesn't need to hear our words or the reasoning that motivated us to merge with all this pain. Though their hands are down now, there is no peace for their unheard thoughts that echo through time.

I continue in spite of age, blackened eyes, dislocated shoulders, and an appearance of having just left the ring. In vain the sun has tried to set on my fading career but my body lives in denial. I box against shadows with more speed than mine. I bob and weave, turn and move. I'm in and I'm out but they are always one step ahead. Deep down I hear the bell that signifies the end, its sound almost unbearable, so I change gloves, old for new. I said no to who I could have been. Now I'm trying to hang on to what I can be. Only time can stop me.

I'm a fighter and all I know is that most days I'm not where I should be. It seems like I knew that fact from the first time I opened my eyes. Somewhere there was an empty ring waiting to be filled by me and the other who teams with myself to rumble until we turn into fountains of blood. I make my opponents whole by running to the corner of the ring reserved for me. Even if I stayed in my chair, didn't get out of bed and remained in the cage fate built, I would still be a fighter. I move. I duck. I skip. I jump. I rise in this house with this wife and these children in this country without representation and no sign of a candidate to champion my cause. I fight with these hands, eat with this broken jaw. I live this life in this image that came from my mother's milk and is now fixed. This is my place and all that sustains me is here and now. This body offers me a fire that burns in its belly and I pull from its flames hungry children that thank me and run off to play. The road has been long, the battles instructive, but the frustrations still remain. In no way do I pretend to know the outcome, but without apology I go to bed every night and wake every morning a prizefighter.

Struggles set fire to all dreams. Images become engulfed in flames. Words burn. The distance between hope and myself seems to widen, but my weapons stay sharp and ready. We all fight against hunger, from cradle to grave, trying to find a way out of the sentence of nothingness. Luck may shine and years pass fruitfully, but poverty isn't something you remember. It's a thing that remembers you. It stays in your blood, planted in you, and is always present.

There are times in our lives when we consider our mistakes, times when we misread signs and chances we didn't take in hope of another day. We wait for another opportunity to live the dream we know to be a stone's throw away. What shape does age take? Is it the shape of the ageing fighter? Does he take on the form of the man or the boxer? And what kind of shape will he finally be once his glory days are over?

My mind is bound by its own ties and the roaring vibrations of the crowd on the night fists rained in thuds. My space is surrounded by those who love the game and rejoice in physical expression that takes place under glittering lights, in front of questioning cameras and judgemental eyes. The experts sing from safe distances with raised voices over microphones into the air filled with noise, charged with things to come. I've settled nothing and fixed nothing with the wall I built against unarmed attack. My hands have cut through nerve and bone and felled bleeding bodies at my feet. But nothing will be settled until I free my mind and find unexpected peace and the ability to love within my gladiator's heart. But I have no wish for the battle to be over. I have no wish to escape down some profound tunnel. I am too deep in preparation and thought. My eyes stare, fixed on the prize. Smiling, I prepare my hands. I know the ring well. I've stood in its centre during titanic wars with no cause to mourn. It's with my own life that I hunt for hope and fortune but the hour is steadily running out. Courage is mine. I mastered it, wisdom too. I poured my spirit into the wars I fought. I took my wounds with pleasure, confronted the enemy I recognised from within the mirror's reflection and watched him retreat.

We battle with joy from boys all the way to men. You hear our roars from distant stands, fuelled by pride and vanity. But there comes a time when that roar can't travel any further. When it can't reach the height it once reached, it can sink into dejected sadness. My whole life I've lived for the moment. My work was a chain of such moments where all I needed came without looking for it. But now what can I expect? I think of champions and brave souls who fought with pride and achieved glory. They were defined by the spirit with which they fought. We are fighters in our youth. But in the end, what? We follow the courses of our lives until we expire before our time, alone and motionless like large stones with all we've endured. In the end we become too heavy to overcome the problems of gravity. Our bodies fought in rage through fatigue and pain, carried more than human weight in search of fame and fortune. Then we became motionless rocks, propped up by other stones who moved with each other if they moved at all.

Yesterday's promise of glorious days aren't always kept and the life we live is lonely but filled with pleasure and surprise while the fire burns. We endure hardship. We pay our dues by choice. We chase our dreams with human strengths and well-conditioned bodies, without fear. My mind was at peace but there was still a need for more action. Because there was no other place I felt safe, I went back to the ring of melted senses, back to screaming anticipation without defence. Back for more cash and held on to my youth the way a child holds onto a toy. But this is not a game of football. You can't pass the ball when you get tired. Fights stay on my mind. Punches linger, dragging their memory. What is it they want to teach me and who remembers what the heart learnt?

Can the heart be wrong? Thirteen years of preoccupation with the same thing, thirteen years of climbing in and out of the ring with hunger, always hunger, ducking the next punch. Year after year I've been sustained by the pain game. Every year I was going to get fit, but it didn't seem to matter, I could hold my own with anyone, fit or unfit. I memorised moves and went into the ring a man no one could bet against with any certainty.

19

EYES ON THE PRIZE

In January 1998, Scott Welch concentrated on me like a wild animal just released from his cage and watched me collapse under the weight of his hands. Down and dead for eight seconds, then I came back to life, dragging myself awkwardly back to my feet to tame his fury with a two-handed counter-attack. It sent him back against the ropes where I kept him for the remainder of the fight.

Scott and I had a history. I had fought Scott, a former World Title Challenger and British Champion from Brighton, before on the Chris Eubank v Henry Wharton undercard in Manchester's G-Mex as part of a Barry Hearn/Jack Trickett Promotion. Scott won a debatable points decision. He then went on to become British Heavyweight Champion, having beaten the big bad James Oyebola. After our first bout, I went on in 1996 to fight an eliminator for that same dream against south Londoner Julius Francis from the Frank Maloney stable.

Julius had been sent to the States to undergo some stiff training sessions in the DUVA gym, where the likes of Evander Holyfield, Michael Moorer and Pernell 'Sweetpea' Whittaker had been put through their paces. He then came back to Britain and won the Southern Area title. His only loss at that point and his first at domestic level came against Scott Welch. Whilst Francis was making his way up the boxing ladder, I scored an upset in a Maloney show when I ended the big-time career of Peckham's Del Boy, Derek 'Sweet D' Williams. Williams had just lost his Commonwealth and European title belts to Lennox Lewis. If only I'd got to him earlier. I was looking to score a double upset. I entered Francis' sweating dream and my bleak and unfriendly hands tore apart his shaven head. I was determined, used my high guard to swallow up distance between the two of us. One eye was closing, and my corner's attempt to iron out the puffy surface left me with a constant stare during the fight, as if I was physically focusing my mind on the campaign ahead. That night seemed to define struggle for me; raising my arms in victory, but having to look ahead to the next stage of my dream.

I didn't get to realise my hope that time; Welch decided not to defend the title against me and went instead for the easier option, that old fossil Joe Bugner out in Germany, all for the money. In a cruel and ironic twist, Welch vacated the title to fight for Henry Akinwande's WBO belt and Francis, with Frank Maloney behind him, picked up the vacant belt. Francis famously went on to fight Iron Mike Tyson. I couldn't call it a fight – he took a beating from the Iron Man right here on my doorstep at the MEN Centre.

I was glad of another chance to meet Welch in the ring, having shared 100 rounds of sparring since our last meeting. I took the fight on two days' notice and, apart from the knockdowns, I dominated him easily. Again they gave him the decision. Again a white heavyweight on a Frank Warren promotion won a debatable decision. The referee stood between us waiting for the score-card but instead someone handed him a script written at the ringside. All he had to do was give the appearance of choosing a winner and the judges agreed. I felt like the walls had closed around me as he raised Welch's arms and the crowd booed in disagreement. The shadow of our two fights passed over us like a bird.

Couldn't I have told the post-match reporter how it felt to be cheated? But you can't explain things like these. Instead Welch faced the press looking full of pain and tired, as if his life had been hard. I felt like saying, 'Don't waste your life complaining, Scott. The show just started, who knows how long it will last, just sit down and enjoy what's left.' He was already a wealthy man outside the boxing ring. I felt no anger towards Welch. I liked him a lot. Though we fought hard to win, he was just another man that life had driven down the path of pain and fatigue. We would meet again in Dublin to spar under the watchful eye of new trainer and former Middleweight Champion Steve Collins, who had twice beaten both Nigel Benn and Chris Eubank. Our hands got to know each other well through those years. Today I alone continue the fight. Scott has no need for the ring. I'm sure we'll meet again at some boxing show where our hands will come together with no trouble at all. They will take delight in the memories of fight nights when they got to know each other. Sixteen fingers and four thumbs will catch up on a lifetime's work in a moment.

I remember before the fight I planned never to fight again, but these hands have taught me to believe in dreams. Proud knuckles, ten friends, furious fellows who move with such blinding speed that they become blurred. A lack of funds meant they submitted themselves once more to the pain they had fallen in love with. But I'm not complaining. I'm just examining the road I travelled to here, the road that won't allow me to waste my life.

Another night, another Frank Maloney contender. Angela sat at the ringside waiting. She didn't care much for the other fights on the undercard. The first fight ended and the score-cards came out but I don't think she understands the first thing about scoring a fight. She became interested in boxing when we began our relationship. She liked the poetry of the struggle, fighters fighting for their one shot at glory. Angela sat with my manager and was well on the way to being merry. Ready to scream down the arena, as always. Her voice often travelled above the crowds. It could cross all the silence of a fighter's world, pass through the centre of noise to put her heart next to his.

I came out exposed, and ended the career of Kevin McBride. He was the Irish Heavyweight Champion, from Barry McGuigan's hometown of Clones. Everything fell into place for this bout. The previous fights had left water all over the canvas. There were patches of blood and spit, very slimy when it gets on the soles of your boots. I was in the middle of throwing a punch and lost my footing. I knew that he had thrown a punch at the same time but it didn't touch me. I just slipped, or so I thought. So why was I hurting? I wasn't sure what was real and what wasn't. So I began to pay more attention. I took my time to consider his every action, while remaining on guard, watchful of which hand had harmed me. I had filled my lungs with expectation of a hard night's work and, as I had anticipated, this guy was slaughtering my body with hard shots. I was being chopped down like a tree when I noticed him linger for what must have been a fraction of a second in slow motion. That was all it took. I exploded on his glass jaw with all I had left. He tried very hard to stay on his feet but his legs refused him and opted instead to perform a break-dancing routine before falling for the fans.

No one understood that at that point he felt absolute loneliness. No one understood the empty place he inhabited between pain, the sound of the bell and the love of his family. How it pleased the crowd to see him stumble into the nothingness of their noise, into a waiting dream. He took his leave of light and soared through the lonely darkness to a silent star. Here pompous referees are quick to penalise with a wink to the promoter and a battered man has no name once the crowd resume their chatter. Someone's dream is ended. Here was a man looking up at the shadow which had caught him and ended his dream. He knew he was finished.

Angela was sober now after sitting through the rounds of what turned out to be an easy fight with McBride. She waited outside my dressing room. I came out. We kissed and went home. I'd come through another ordeal intact. But I felt tired of the fight I lived for. Tired of raising weary arms only to watch them fall detached from my intentions. Tired of the hands that searched my face in order to find and defeat me. Fed up with training and mastering skills. There are always men sitting at the ringside waiting for the action to begin, circling around the pain offered them. I'm tired of their lust for blood and their corrupt indifference. I just played my part. Maybe I would outlive this feeling and have it explained to me. The voice of Phil Martin, my late trainer, came eerily to mind.

'Feelings have no place in a fighter's world,' he would always tell me. 'I'd wake up in the mornings and sometimes I didn't feel like going to work but I'd go because that's my job.'

He would explain the distinction between a coward and a hero, beginning with the question. 'What's the difference between the two?'

Its familiarity meant that I wouldn't forget the right answer and often wondered why he'd even bothered to ask. 'The hero does his job,' I'd answer quickly. 'Phil, we've been through this a thousand times.'

'Exactly,' he'd say and continue as if I hadn't spoken, 'They both feel the same but the coward is beaten by his own feelings of fear, doubt or of whatever and runs away. The hero does his job. A soldier fights, a fireman runs into burning buildings etc. Not because of how they feel but because of duty, self-control, pride and discipline. Your feelings will change; it's natural. They come to life and they fade away for reasons unknown.'

Frank Maloney got his own back for my upsets over his fighters by choosing me to fight John Ruiz. Ruiz is now the WBC World Heavyweight Champion, having beaten and taken the title from Evander 'The Real Deal' Holyfield, over twelve rounds. Our bout was to be in Ipswich in May 1998. I drove down with Jack Trickett, Michael Brodie (former European Bantamweight Champion and World Title Challenger) and our trainer at the time, Ray Farrell. We arrived very late, around midnight, and Maloney hadn't booked us in separately. The hotel was full except for one room. Jack and Ray slept on the floor and Brodie and myself shared the one double bed, sleeping head to toe. I was woken by the unmistakable smell of trainer feet as Brodie's foot seemed ·clamped to my face.

John Ruiz was known as the quiet man. He seemed like an animal, surrounded by silence. He was from an isolated, humble and intelligent breed. He avoided all contact with me at the weigh-in, which I misread as a lack of confidence. But now I know that dangerous men don't stand on the tops of buildings spitting and swearing. Silence was his victory; it gave nothing away.

Ruiz was a counter-puncher who relied on his quickness. He was fast. He had to be a good fighter because I wasn't in the mood to lose to anyone. For me it would have been a career-defining win. It was clear from the opening bell that he wanted one thing, my body. The man from Puerto Rico had technical ability I'd never faced before. He had the strategy to come in and box with me, waiting for me to make a mistake and capitalise off those errors with devastating body punches. I had taken the fight on three or four days' notice, as usual, and had never heard of or seen John Ruiz before that night. Nice one, Maloney!

By now I was focusing more and more on my age, worrying about dying slowly, concerned I'd missed too many opportunities. It seemed increasingly that I would never fly, always be rooted to this piece of ground. I worried that someone else would take Angela from me, and that I would end up as nothing more than an inaccessible thought in the heads of my children. Some of us still remain clear and unaffected by years of pounding fists, willing to talk about our dazed and punchy friends. So young warriors will find themselves moved by the recollections of the ring and the shared respect that gladiators earned from one another. I've been lucky enough to pass through decades of fistfights in one piece and able to bear witness. I turned myself into something I understood and tried to make all I could of myself. The battle-dress I put on was the right one. I was recognised as the person I thought I was. No one contradicted me. The mask fitted so I wore it but when I wanted to take the mask off, it was stuck to my face. When I finally removed it and saw myself in the mirror I had already grown old.

THE JOURNEYMAN

20

BACKGROUND ARTIST

I wanted to go back to my birth and to begin again. I was tired of this body, tied to other opponents in a string of fights. I was ready to put away the dream of a child, the whirlwind vision that had picked me up and taken me on a journey to the arena. I had learned about another body, confident, strong, master of itself. I learned to dance with my hands high, turning and making angles until opponents became still. I had bathed in the vision I had of myself, soaked my body in my own splendour. I was the fist that broke the jaws of like-minded dreamers. I turned canvas floors into lakes of blood, then returned home with blackened eyes, where my woman would ignite me with a sparkling kiss like a gentle breeze grazing through my eyelashes.

I was tired of this illusion and the lonely hours of training. When would the dream be over? I was planted in this dust, this earth, a seed among the battle-dead and born again into a warrior's life. I was rained on and given sun and water in a field ploughed by a million cheering fans, as a gladiator who cut off breathing and removed living hearts from fighting men. The world honours such men. I would continue to compete against them and take their hearts in a lightning flash. Although in my navel the whirlwind grows calm, head wounds have begun to heal, tears have run dry and the pain that was born with me has left me to inhabit another, I don't know where it will end. I'll just go as far as I can. After so many wins and losses all that's left is Michael Murray, heavyweight, nobody.

I was already teaching some music. What other options were there? I could become a trainer of other nobodies. Or teach celebrities who think that fighters are glamorous and want to feel tough by hitting someone else; I could teach someone like that how to hide from his reality, giving him the reassurance that makes him feel safe. I could explain that tough is a boy beaten to the ground who gets up repeatedly saying 'Come on then!' Taught by a father to take his punishment without self-pity, a father who ends up an opponent when the bell rings.

I began working as a television extra, a background artist. It aroused in me a deep fantasy of stardom, plausible in a dream world but not really in mine. I worked on *Brookside* at Merseyside TV, *At Home with the Braithwaites* at Yorkshire TV, *Cold Feet* at Granada TV and I played a builder on *Coronation Street* for quite a while. I perfected a new kind of silent waiting, different to the kind before a match. Waiting for the director who had shouted 'Take' and to then shout 'Cut, that's a wrap!'

Picture this. It's the final scene and I'm sat on this bus drowning in coffee for what seems like forever. There's a spider on the window that's been here even longer. It's not moving but I know it's alive. The lights remain on, which means filming in progress. Now it's even quieter. If you listen closely you can hear the cameras breathing. The lights go off, the extras are called and put into their positions, finally the moment we'd been waiting for all day. The director shouts 'Action!' and we fill out the background by sitting or walking around. Whether we speak or just give the appearance of speaking, stardom for us is definitely far from a reality. Who are we portraying in the background? Other people, the people that we forget about in our everyday lives, except to recall how insignificant they were in the drama of our own lives.

Being part of television was the complete opposite of boxing. Television portrays life through reflection. It's just an abstraction of our self-awareness. All we derive from it is the need to see ourselves. How many hours do we spend focused only on the illusion of our lives, the dreamed past or the imaginary future, while the present vegetates on the couch? Here we are calm with no reason, free from challenge, watching a portrayal of our lives acted out on-screen. Histories are made and the search for still undiscovered oceans continues. Brief seconds, minutes, hours while away. Hopes are unattained on this stage of real life, the stage outside of that box where we watch living dreams. The best examples I knew of this were the stalkers, autograph hunters, camped outside studios with naked feet swollen from hours of waiting. Even though they seem gentle and tame, actors flee from their dangerous passions. One gets the feeling that if the fans caught their celebrity, their dresses or their shirts would be torn from their backs, all because they're on television.

In 1998 I also started playing music live again, that beautiful illusion, the seductive dream rooted in my head. The ecstasy, that mixture of rhythm, dynamics and harmony which always forced my body into movement. Music had always been an expert healer that tended to my wounds, offered me warm comfort. It overwhelmed me with the joy of the moment, gave me the will to live on in order to experience more.

After years of broken jaws, lost teeth and torn lips, I had changed instruments from trumpet to guitar. The guitar had a single head and six strings. Nothing more than a body and a neck that ended in sound. Behind every string there was another that was plucked and another which sang, all making beautiful sounds in transparent air. Sharps and flats conspired in whispers, then clung to each other for brief moments, repeating the same sounds, the same sounds. On certain chords they glowed and glittered. For me, the guitar's music conjured up another world, different to boxing, where the bright lights of fame and fortune always shine. Women are always sharp,

THE JOURNEYMAN

157

luxurious cars always fast, and contracts are always signed at crossroads where agents appear in empty cars amidst the dust and the whispers of unseen passengers.

I always enjoy the full, rounded bass sound of Jaco Pastorius' Fender. It was a sound that just enjoyed being. A strong, never-disappointing vibration of air that carried joy, a joy that recalled past joys. It must have been a pleasure beyond his physical being. A love and understanding of music that didn't come from thinking. Thinking destroys because it clashes with its creative self and moves an artist farther away from joy. Jaco knew this and lived in the moment.

I walked into the smoked-filled atmosphere of the Band on the Wall Club in Manchester, into a jam before dawn with masters of sound and air. As I walked in, rhythms of the past came screaming into my body. I looked over hundreds of detached heads moving in synchronisation to a pulse and saw a lone bassist unknown to me standing on a stage as though that's where he lived and would always live. He reminded me of Jaco. His rhythm moved with so many things in our lives that it was a miracle that anyone who heard him didn't just break down and cry. I heard a tempo that made such an impression on me that, without realising it, I lost myself in it. The beat seemed to become inseparable from the one in my own chest. Even though the encounter is distant now, it is still fused, dissolved in my pulse. A wave of time dissected and calculated the thoughts that surged from my head to my chest and installed itself there like a throbbing that could never be satisfied.

The air was pregnant with sounds that invaded my head, saxophones roaring like wounded animals. I sank my hand into my guitar case and pulled out my Yamaha six-string bass, to defend myself against the horns. Without fanfare I take on the fierce beat. We changed keys and spiralled down an octave into another dawn, into the chorus, through a wake of fifth circles, wind forced from lungs through metal. Then a solo ended, touching down like a tired bird after a long flight. Not wanting to play for the sake of playing, our silence split time into two. A moment later two notes. Then many more meeting in a phrase that no one player dictated. They ignited and burned, eventually going out never to be repeated.

Jazz, like boxing, lives in the moment, with no room for nostalgia. New combinations of notes are right now preparing to move into action. I wasn't hoping for anything that wasn't already there. One has talent if there is talent, opportunity if you seek opportunity and luck if it's granted. I put all that I could into playing the bass guitar, all that time allowed. After the jam I was asked by the organisers if I wanted to take part in open jam sessions that would last a week in Hamburg, Germany, as part of a rhythm section made up of other musicians from around Europe.

We are all moving steadily through the years. Who's winning, who's keeping score? Those on their journey don't seem to show interest in anyone else's travels. I was moving forward to a new and very different life, and was equally guilty of not caring about other people's movements, be they forward or backward. My thoughts were occupied with my own survival, my own hunger, the fight, the music. I took the gig not knowing where it might lead and left for Germany.

21

HAMBURG

Angela drove me towards Manchester Airport. The journey kept reeling us in to our destination at a steady speed until the trance of driving made all the roads appear as one. We arrived at our journey's end. I was booked on a flight to Hamburg, where I would be taking part in a week of open jam sessions. I picked up my ticket at the desk and in the last minutes before leaving we spoke almost more than on the ride up.

'You'll be in Hamburg in a couple of hours so phone me as soon as you get there. Love you.'

We kissed and I left. At the other end of my journey, on German soil, I was taken aside and everything was pure interrogation. 'What's your business here in Germany? Where were your parents born? Are you African? Did you pack your own bags? Where are you staying in Germany?'

Then a rifle motioned me to move. With a guarded and apparent nonchalance, I followed obediently. I collected my bags, replaced the contents and was freed from airport security to continue the journey to my hotel.

This was my second visit to Hamburg. The first came some years earlier when I came at a few days' notice to fight the WBO

Cruiserweight Champion Markus Bott, a local of Hamburg. I fought him right here in his own backyard and I knocked him out in the seventh round. I've fought all over Germany, east and west. Men like Timo Hoffman and Willi Fischer. German boxing fans always remember and recognise me because of the fight with Bott and they often approach me for autographs. At the time of beating Bott, their hero, I thought they were going to lynch me. However, the Germans, though gutted, took the defeat like gentlemen and showed me a lot of respect.

The first time I came to Hamburg I was with Herbie Hide, the former WBO Heavyweight Champion from Norwich, Eamonn Loughran, a former Welterweight Champion from Northern Ireland, and Barry Hearn's chauffeur to name but a few. Barry and Jack Trickett would join us later on fight night. I spent my time sitting around the hotel with Loughran talking boxing, waiting for the weigh-in, focused on fighting, while Hide and the chauffeur cruised and got to know the streets of Hamburg. So even though I'd been here before I was ignorant of the side of the city that Hide and the chauffeur got to know all too well. When I explained to Hide that sex would weaken his legs before a fight, he told me that oral sex didn't affect him.

I almost believed him after the way he beat up his former sparring partner, Eddie Gonzalez, the following night. Gonzalez was a heavy-drinking Mexican roadsweeper whom Hide trained with every day at the Matchroom Gym in Romford. I'd also worked with Hide there from time to time. The fight against Gonzalez was an absolute liberty but then again southern fighters are spoon-fed opponents for them to knock out throughout their careers and are always found wanting when it comes to a real test. A live opponent is a completely different experience.

As I picked up my gig bag, night was falling and people were going home, to work or for a night out. My hotel was in walking distance of the club where I jammed. As I walked I thought of the tremendous contrast between the two worlds of night and day. This was the hour which I associated with the colour red; it always evoked many thoughts and feelings for me. It was very different to that unconscious world of the fighter lying in a pool of blood, his keen body trained to precision and his bound hands and heart lying still. It used to be there that my night would begin. But here in Hamburg the people were full of colours, all distinct.

There were little bars filled almost exclusively with women of the night, their pimps, thugs and johns. It wouldn't matter how often you passed, thinking you wouldn't enter their reality, they would eventually invite you in at a price. As sordid as you may have felt it to be, you'd become attached and one night find your whole life transformed by its fantasy. But this was a sex market, with its ups and downs, like any other exchange. There, assured of the night, women brought their generous supplies to benefit those who lived their lives in fantasies of ravished furs and bold, predatory eyes. Prostitutes strolled the streets craving the attention of their public. They must have been noticed as they stalked all males through days that passed into empty nights.

A perfect voice sang beautiful songs for all those who entered The Jive Club. We musicians lured the listener into a spiritual space, conveying delicately structured thoughts. An everlasting assessment of those souls whose insistent pulse commented on glorious times. Scattered chords stretched, unbroken by the clatter of beer glasses and whispered conversations. Music was a love that spoke telepathically, melodies and harmonies conveyed through syncopated air. In their flight, transparent dots from a page culminated in one vibrant breath; the interpreted dream of a new octave was carried by bars from the world of sleep to that of waking. The drums translated time into fractions of moments; they bore their heart's rhythm through the commitment of agile sticks, striking a clear direction of the sound to follow. The blues bled infinitely on those nights, seemingly holding music beyond time.

In Hamburg live jazz could often be found where bright red drew eyes to lost mornings and oceans of sperm-filled strange rubber.

Steadily, secret fantasies beat their monotonous rhythms through districts of stone flesh. Pimps mingled in the bars that were harbours of fantasies and pussy. Their eyes were always on the prowl, as they waited with unspoken prices, hidden in the night's innermost darkness. On the street, whores conceded dialogue with unquestioning eyes that smiled. Their undeniably vast experiences moved onwards with the long procession of johns. I saw how their moving hips swayed in the night and quickened, while their penniless palms passed through car windows, sweating with the desire for more cash.

There was a fetish club next door to the bar where the jam sessions took place. There consenting adults whipped each other, warm blood was exposed to cracking leather, and harnessed creatures were roped and confined with precision. The first night I arrived, a full moon allowed me to examine the club's surroundings in more detail. I was astonished to recognise the club, matching it with a memory in my mind's eye. Deep in the basement was a gym I'd used in preparation for the fight with Markus Bott. It was identical to the first gym I trained in back in Manchester's red-light district on Chorlton Street. I had wandered down into the belly of that club many times, a cold shadow always following me to the moist, chilly and dim basement. A small electric heater drew out damp from the walls. It was a tiny dungeon that divided into a ring area, four or five punchbags in a corner, a skipping area and a floor mat for groundwork and sit ups. The room couldn't hold more than a dozen people.

Hamburg brought together many poor and desperate people. I always thought of children weeping in their desolate homes, eyes beholding the vicious circle of their futures. Boys turned to sport or crime; girls to early motherhood and/or prostitution. Sometimes music and drugs brought the two groups together again. It seemed an undefined place where shrunken souls had to set their own rules in order to leave. A place where in afternoons past I began my work.

With the sex trade constantly busy on those streets, it was easy to forget that entertainment also took place in the jazz clubs. The music swung without end, the wind carried hot sounds and dreams that climbed subtle changes. I knew what took me there. The steady beat was wedged in my soul, beyond the reach of a prostitute's appeal. No point focusing on the constant wandering of eyes or the shadowed pieces of flesh. Their hearts beat a dark tempo that synchronised with the rhythms of the street.

My week's engagement was as part of the rhythm section at The Jive. The music is always live there, and the horns climbed higher and higher, demanding an audience's attention. If you can find it, the music never stops playing. Yes, you would pass the women in windows: mannequins with their prices set in their minds, their breath cold and voices numb, articulately haggling with the johns. But the moment people entered that club their heads bounced, their knees bent and their hips swung. This was the music they came for. The crowd had a simple curiosity: to hear musicians whose instruments were extensions of their bodies; to watch the way they held the horns, the bass, as if they were alive and could escape from the band. My bass lines played as if I was walking on a cold winter's day, taking small steps. Glad to be playing and feeling like an important part of the music. A bass can forget its role: walk too fast or stand too still. Then the music ran off or floated over the audience. The crowd's eyes would enjoy watching those small steps I took. You'd have thought my bass was in love and that Angela was waiting backstage, a fur coat covering her sensual, naked body.

As always, a thousand shadows took to the dance floor and swayed from foot to foot with rhythmic fluidity and perfect grace. Surrounding the floor strange harmonic creatures sat patiently at tables just enjoying the horns that blew from an open stage. There phrases flowed in straight lines, backed by chosen chords. Lovers came to hear notes of joy and their desire was the magnet from which the jazz hung. Sometimes it seemed like their kisses controlled the tides raising the floodgates for the music to burst through.

My fingers stretched down a long neck, plucking invisible sounds that echoed over the brush strokes of soft drums that gave the darkness its pulse. The songs we played were sung by wind all at once in a single phrase, a phrase that tied us to life's joy. The sounds they heard came from friends. Blue sounds that said it all and there was still time to hear more, time to feel fingers on a fretboard moving faster than your eyes could see. They heard arrangements taking spontaneous flight. The armies of freed notes extracted from my brass heart, recognisable airs that fell on half-closed eyes. I could have stayed there and been happy between the rhythms of bass and drums. I heard a chord enter above ledger lines. I moved upon an octave and dived headlong into its sound. A new key changed the shape of the line above creation. Then the music was saying everything. Did they understand how the message was thought up then written and played for them in one living moment? The Germans heard the right notes struck and said, 'Wow, that's great music!'

One night as I left the club I saw a crowd gathering across the street. A violent argument had erupted and brutal statues squared up. A name was called off a stranger's tongue. I think it was a pimp's name, deliberately spoken. The pimp who protects his girl, works her, drops her, then returns with a customer to penetrate her beyond pain. They were just workers of a street darkly lit, creating a red dawn. They had intricate habits and a price that rose in whispers. They were barren of conventional morality. Reserve your pity for them and not for those johns who hurried through the streets leaving behind hungry fatherless homes that waited faithfully in vain for their return. Though they may remember a fleeting joy mounted on a whore with their testicles emptied, the memory would become bitter with passing time.

A feast of strangers is entertained by lesbian exhibitions behind the city's red-light districts. Jazz bars give their own personal assurances of enjoyment, smiles included. Love's tortured music in all its shades of blue never fades out. A lust for something and a lust for nothing, there is a need to relax and listen to plucked strings that vibrate long after the crowd has gone. Then comes the fading of sound whilst shadowy dreamy hours move at a lazy pace. It is possible to dream while listening to the right phrase, the one that simply captivates you.

In the space of one week, I tried to reach that stage of perfection where rhythm, time, melody and harmony fused with audience and performance. It must be like great sex or drugs. One night I decided to break my abstinence from pot and search for a high like Miles Davis used to. Agile fingers crumbled fragments of dried weed. I folded the paper, sealed it with a wet tongue and let time slide.

The audience seemed to admire me that night, even though I lacked any real plan. Everything came by ear. I created dreams from the bottom of a cruel high, walking the bridge in four-four time, changing chords towards absolute beauty. In the end it all seemed too much for the audience to keep up with – where the hell was the melody? Many feet counted time under small tables while swarms of images fluttered around their half-closed eyes. Then a bird took centre stage, wires entangled around his ankles. Heads fell with the sound of his horn. His sound pecked at their souls as they surrendered to his will. Everything sang, everything was sound, everything was prepared to contribute to the music. Suddenly there was a pause: a silent end to the night. The band left the stage and it was time to go home, back to sunny Manchester. Or was that rainy Manchester?

THE JOURNEYMAN

167

22

FRANKFURT

The evening was calm, the normally trembling air breathed sweetly and played soft, gentle of spirit, though discontented with my long fruitless employment. A few hours had passed since arriving home from Germany. I'd spent them trying to disentangle myself from the embrace of needs, the kids' needs, the car's needs, my wife's needs, but there's no escaping the need to pay bills. They all seemed to be pacing around me like a threatening shadow. The phone rang. I answered. It was Jack Trickett. Hearing his voice conjured the vision of that old familiar face.

'Mike, there's a fight in Frankfurt on Saturday with Danny Williams. It's a ten-rounder. Do you want it?'

Today was Thursday, I hadn't trained for weeks. Danny Williams was considered to be the best heavyweight in the country apart from Lennox Lewis. I thought for a second. 'If you utter a figure I understand,' I said and immediately threw yesterday behind me.

I didn't even have the time to think of today, it was already tomorrow. I could see his face. I didn't have the time to refresh mine. As is often the case when I've a fight at short notice, I turned to my own strength. There was no time to prepare for my next prospect. Williams grew up as a fighter. He had punching power. He'd proven that to me years earlier on the undercard of a Prince Naseem show in Manchester when he caught me cold and the referee stopped me from replying to a decent enough right hand. Williams has a good temperament. A British Muslim from Brixton, south London, he now holds the British and Commonwealth titles.

Williams' trainer, Jim McDonald, the former European Featherweight Champion, had worked with former opponents of mine like Scott Welch and Herbie Hide. He'd worked in their corners and knew me well. Frank Warren was the show's promoter. He was expecting big things from Williams, the latest prize stallion from his stables. In my mind he was there to be damaged by me, not to fulfil Warren's own need for self-justification. The fulfilment of my needs lay in my own hands. Yes, I was out of shape. I had no conditioning, hadn't trained properly in weeks, I was too busy trying to be a musician. I am a fighter. I had experience, I had heart and I loved a good tear-up. A fighter in the truest senses should be able to go anywhere at anytime and hold his own. That's his job.

I was taken from Frankfurt Airport straight to the weigh-in. There was no time to pause, to ease the load, take a rest, a quiet intake of breath or simply close my eyes for a minute. As some kind of promotional idea, the weigh-in took place in a shopping centre in front of hundreds of shoppers. They watched as two dozen fighters got on and off the scales in front of media from around the globe. Photographers swarmed and journalists hustled for interviews. The British claimed their space by taking over a small café. I heard Williams telling Glen McCrory, part of the Sky Sports team, that having just got back from sparring in America he was in great shape. I doubted it, he'd just weighed-in at well over 18 st.

There were a lot of familiar names on the bill that night. Richie Woodhall, the former Super-middleweight Champion from Telford was there. I'd been on Richie's undercard when Markus Beyer had challenged him for his belt. My opponent that night had been Rene Monse, the German Heavyweight Champion. Woodhall had given everything to hold on to his title but Beyer looked sensational that

THE JOURNEYMAN

night. Now it was Glen Catley's turn to take it to the German in Frankfurt. He was from Bristol and also a Super-middleweight. He was topping the bill. Catley had been robbed in a WBC title challenge against Woodhall in Telford but Woodhall, like a true warrior, having been given the decision told the camera and press, 'I lost that fight!' Woodhall's opponent this night was Nottingham's Errol McDonald.

The years had reclaimed McDonald's ferocity, time taking back whatever he foolishly thought he had. There is a perpetual struggle inside and outside of all of us; a hostile environment that will eventually reclaim you to its eternal silence. When George Foreman became the oldest man to win the Heavyweight title at age 45 he was still young. After becoming the youngest man at the age of 17 to win a world title, Wilfred Benitez became old in his early 20s. In boxing years one can be old at 20 or young at 50. Old is when you're walking on your heels, when you can no longer absorb punishment. When your reflexes have slowed to the point where you're unable to get out of the way of punches. When you can no longer defend yourself in the boxing ring. When your words are no longer decipherable. Errol McDonald was old and we all knew it.

After their fight I asked Richie Woodhall how he had gone on against McDonald. He said, 'I felt terrible, McDonald had nothing, he wasn't even competitive. I didn't want to hit him.' Woodhall even looked upset. I liked him even more.

He had lived the wars unaccompanied. He wasn't claiming to know the master-plan or pretending to have a comprehensive understanding of life and the strategies of others, but he knew McDonald should not have been in the ring with a young fit warrior like himself. He had an awareness and an intelligence I never expected.

A true warrior shakes the hand of his victor no matter what referees, judges or anyone else tells them. I remember I fought Matthew Ellis from Blackpool. I dropped him three times and he knew who the winner was. Deep down we always do. But once the

THE JOURNEYMAN

referee raised his arm and gave him the decision he claimed my victory. He has recently signed a contract with the two Franks, Warren and Maloney, and is now fronting like the next white hope. Another example is Noel Quarless, who was booed in his hometown of Liverpool when they gave him the decision. He accepted the victory that denied me a shot at Lennox Lewis early in our careers. He was knocked out by Lewis in round two. I was in Germany with Michael Sprott from Reading once and when asked by a trainer who had won a fight we'd had in Bethnal Green he couldn't answer. I had to answer for him, 'You were given the decision.'

Sprott knew that he'd run like a rabbit and held on like a dancer. Even his own corner, the very respected Terry Lawless, Frank Bruno's old trainer, told him he'd lost the fight. I knew that if I hadn't been there he would've had no problem claiming my victory.

I almost fought Pele Reid. The bell rang; we came together. He threw a punch that missed. I threw a punch and dislocated my shoulder. Nine seconds later the fight was over. Anywhere else in the world that would've been called a no-contest. But Reid claimed the victory, saying that he had punched my shoulder out of its socket. When Barry McGuigan played the tape back it was clear that no one had landed a punch and he was a liar.

Richie Woodhall was the first guy I heard say, 'I've been given the decision but I lost the fight.' For that he became a hero, a man of honour, a true warrior, a human being with integrity and a sense of fair play. What honour can there be in claiming another man's victory? What obscures a man's vision to the point that he is prepared to annihilate pride in bad judgement? Without pride how can this be a noble art fought by gentlemen?

The night before the fight with Danny Williams I had locked myself out of my hotel room while asking Bob Shannon, my trainer, what time we were having breakfast. His room was opposite. I'd just got out of the shower and only had a towel on. Williams was in the corridor. He saw me and asked what the problem was. I told him and he offered to go down to reception for a new key. He came back, handed me the key and said, 'Goodnight.' I tried hard to see an ulterior motive for this kindness, but there was none. I found only innocence. How could I consider that my enemy? He was just a decent human being who wanted to help, even if that person wanted to destroy him.

During the fight I felt slow; my midriff no longer danced with muscle. I lacked movement but my anticipation was good. He began an endless and vigorous hunt for my head. He deserted all his skill. My plan was to do nothing for six rounds, let him tire then take him in the four remaining rounds. As long as he continued head-hunting that would've worked. He was hitting nothing with big left hooks and wild right hands. Everything went to plan for four rounds. What do they say about best-laid plans? The fifth round revived old desires. I began to dig them up again from where I'd last buried them. I woke up and decided to take the fight into the trenches. This was real, there was nowhere to hide from dangerous hands or the vision of the prize in sight. A vision that engaged secret dreams. Dreams I knew could burn stretched out in lactic acid across the canvas that covered a waiting abyss, like the skin of the drum beating in my chest. To have the ability to change the fight plan in the heat of battle shows real class, flexibility and intelligence, that's what I saw. Williams at 18.5 st got up on his toes and started boxing. Where the hell did that come from? Then he closed my right eye with a jab.

I came out of the sixth round with one eye completely closed. He immediately took advantage, throwing left hooks to my soft belly, one of which cut off my breathing. Air left my lungs and its absence deformed my features. Blood rushed through my veins in search of oxygen. Thoughts took leave of absence and tore childhood dreams from their roots. 'Good shot!' I told him and set to throw my own left hook. The best punch to throw against a hook is another, hoping your opponent has dropped his right hand and left his chin exposed. I wanted him to see the trap and back off, giving me time to catch my breath. I thought it had worked when he took half a step backwards, I relaxed. It hadn't worked. He jumped in with a big hook to my midsection. The pain swept through my body before doubling me over. The referee stopped the fight and gave Williams his victory.

The fight of the night was Glen Catley v Marcus Beyer for the WBC Super-middleweight title. Catley was fighting an aggressive fight, bobbing and weaving, always going forward, hustling Beyer out of the counter-punching role he like to be in. He was clearly winning and the fight was almost at an end but Beyer was still there and still looked strong.

I had spoken to Catley earlier and said, 'Glen, listen. I fought Willi Fischer [Willi Fischer was a former World Title challenger] here in Frankfurt. I watched him break-dance and body-pop every time I landed a punch. I spent the night beating him up. He wasn't a problem, but now I understand that if you fight a German in his own country and especially in his own town all he has to do to win is hear the final bell still standing.'

When Catley came out for the 12th I was beginning to fear the worst. Then suddenly Catley landed a peach of a punch that laid Beyer out for the full count. There were no more than two dozen British watching and yet our sound travelled above 40,000 German fans. It was fantastic. The Germans wanted collectively to hide, especially the promoter. His head was on the line. Catley was supposed to have been an easy first defence for Beyer. I had nothing against Marcus Beyer: we had often met in Cologne when I sparred with the big German champion Timo Hoffman. Beyer was a gentleman.

Before I left the stadium a few members of the German press came over to me and asked, 'Michael Murray, when are you going to get a German passport?'

I laughed and replied, 'I speak English and Spanish. English by birth and Spanish by choice. I would hate to have to learn German it's much too . . .' (ugly came to mind) ' . . . difficult.'

They laughed.

23

HOME

dreamt about another mind in another body. A different paradise, unlike the council estate I live on where tenants retch and vomit in disgust, where new blood bares its teeth in resentment while drowning in its own tears. Where aspirations slide deeper into shattered dreams, only to be thrown up again by the old people who forget to wipe the sick from their faces before coming out to play with our children. On the streets where children throw fists and stones, running in rags while they roar like tigers. With muscles of iron, they throw mud in the faces of barking dogs. Dogs who turn and run after them, looking into the burning eyes of a child without mercy. Children of broken homes with single parents, children in houses without floors to lay carpets on and nobody to say I love you.

Could it be possible that I may always live like this, growing old where the tenants have nothing? Can it ever be too late to create a dream and make it happen? There are many around here who are happy to settle for what they have, long established patterns of comfort. They have already settled for nothing. As long as the world remains as it is people are happy to remain as they are. I live in Gorton, here my thoughts buzz round all the things I own (a stereo and my Yamaha bass guitar) or should I say the material things that matter to me. My fists are sought but my feet drag in the boredom of the wasted talents I know I have.

I stare at my footsteps and deny them, walking like a strange person in the streets of my home around bloodstained flowers laid for children murdered by children. Any person is more at home here than I am. The walls and the wind withdraw obediently from my skin. I breathe in the bitter air of anyone looking at me. Peeling off my afro I expel me, then breathe me in along with my history.

A history of living on an estate just like this, where blazing hands darkened the skyline with German salutes, and ignoble hearts beat with the blood of hate as they circulated their filth. Their howling rhythms could be heard along with wild barking dogs in the street, roaring with rage. Violence spread from one edge of the world to another. They called themselves the National Front and spewed their sickness onto my street with screaming venom, ready to stomp a Nigger or a Jew into darkness. The minorities answered in different tongues and struggled for life amongst shaven-headed opposition and Union Jacks. Their cries for help went untranslated. Now I see ignorance as a dying pulse. The heart declines with its throbbing flood. The streets that once ran red, like an overflowing stream on a battlefield, have grown pale, like the white power of foul fear, now faint in its movement. It has shrunk in size, but like the devil's intensity it still lives. Who doesn't understand hate and ignorance and the silent manifestations of its twisted ideas?

Unseen, down so low in the depths of deprivation, squalid minds in tatters scavenged, searching for an idea that matters: an ideology to be chewed upon with no consequence to heed. They lived among the working classes with nowhere else to feed. Tattoos unseen by soap for months and no hair to comb. Weathered faces of expressionless hate and minds long past lame. Don't be too secure in the knowledge that this world is passing you by. Observation is free but there will be a price to pay. Time is right now holding its watch over you, demanding that you escape the restraint of your tedious routine and look in the mirror that will expect you in vain, before your transparent memory is lost beyond recollection, forgotten by space and time.

My daughter Vienna gave birth to a lovely baby boy she named Malaki. She's young, and because of that I know that one day she'll discover the direction of her own dream, beyond left and right, by focusing on the straight line towards the horizon. Beyond daring, beyond a baby's face consumed by light and joy. I'm too young to be a grandfather in my mid-30s. At 17 I was too young to be a father, though I accepted it. Now Vienna, aged 17, repeats the same cycle with the words, 'Well, you can't say anything because you were only 17 when you had me and grandma was only 14 when she had her first.' She begins again the days I remember. Though I'm sure love will unfold itself and turn towards a baby's new face with words of affection and hope.

Life changes partly because of its own reflection of itself, because of technological advances, ambition, fear, appetite, ageing, love, hope and the journey through wild dilemmas. Life will always be changing but what is really different? To what extent can we recognise signs of something new when everything looks the same? What brings me here too young to remember or forget my life?

Home is a place where the weight of my world is carried on my family's back as is theirs on mine. My battered flesh was betrayed by an indifferent world that exuded a sinister content and believed that a strong mind and heart would pass the test, that all hurt and doubt would dissolve into time. It was wise and I was the fool. Anonymous, unknown, broken-hearted, afraid of the human instincts to love, I sat on a timeless cloud above my life willing to suffer the consequence of loneliness. But there was a slow drizzle down to the weighted world, heavier now than predicted in my youth and I remained a slave to gravity in the world I couldn't change. I changed the things I could and accepted the things I couldn't and began to live knowing that there is no escaping life or death.

I entered through the front door and as I walked in there was no need to look around me. Objects were already fixed in my mind. The response to my arrival was routine. This is where my mind and my heart live. We all understand the private language a family invents. Speech is unnecessary and the need to pretend to be someone else is left at the entrance. The whole house accepts me as part of their reality. This is family. Here I'm secure.

My mother stood at the edge of a shadow that showed her the line that led to and from her children. I saw her image through her dried tears. They fell hot and real throughout wasted years. But now her life has turned around. She must have dug a hole in her heart, cold and dark, and there buried all the pain of a failed marriage and a subsequent relationship. All without words, as Jamaicans do, keeping aloof, her thoughts beyond recall, her silence said what she never would. She was now looking forward to adventure in the Big Apple. I looked once more on the absent face she wore too calmly in front of me. We were both looking in different directions and couldn't shine with the same sun in our eyes. She was ready to spread her wings and fly to America to reunite with her sisters, my aunts, now settled in New York. She smiled bright and bleak like the cold waves she would be crossing, although she would stand firm like an iceberg while all the sea moved around her. There was still an issue of distance and travel between us. She said goodbye, sold everything she owned and gave in to all her weariness.

I admired her strength. It suited her character more than the role of a victim. She was a woman who needed no sight to see that her decision was the right one. To remain would have meant standing still, reducing her will and listening to her own heart ticking loudly on one stalled second. She left for the States and now time is in her pocket. I suspect that we may not see each other again. Our long gaze and last goodbye contained nothing to appease that recognition, nothing at all but a familiar absence that left me feeling half-numbed to face the child in me alone.

My mother has become a traveller, an American explorer. When she looked down from the aeroplane, did she see the American ways of life, people separated from people by what they have in common, or did she just see lights, street lamps, illuminated skyscrapers, headlights and darkness? Wherever I spoke from or in what particular voice, my thoughts went with her. The law of distance meant that my thoughts travelled through smoky air but changed her tune in silence. The traveller knocked on her family's moonlit door and met cousins, brothers and sisters. My mother must have been over the moon to see them.

At night I imagine my mother taking out her false teeth and placing them in a glass of water. She doesn't eat any more. Taking out her tongue and wrapping it in a towel. She no longer talks. Her arms and legs, knotted together, have stopped moving. She curls up like a child in bed. After she has taken off the thoughts it has taken her a lifetime to learn, she takes off England. When she takes off everything all that's left is a wish for a better life. America is a blind wish, though the wish isn't blind. Maybe the hope will see what it wants to see. Dreams happen in the dark shadows of life while we are sleeping. Around her, her brothers and sisters are sleeping but there are no children, at least not her own.

I have four sisters and one brother. The eldest, Audrey, my half-sister, I knew nothing of until I came back to England. She disliked me immediately. I still have no idea why. My presence irritated her. I could always sense her anger but could never put my finger on her bitterness. She's a single parent. Has a good job, nice home and three children: two girls, Toni and Natasha, and a boy, Junior. I used to send them half-eaten boxes of chocolate for Christmas wrapped with a card. I'd take out my favourites (I'm a sucker for hazelnut whips) and empty the rest into the box. They knew every year they were from Uncle Mike. I had the right intention but I always seemed to be broke and hungry. If I'd ever received anything in return I would have felt really guilty. Christmas is a time to remember those less fortunate than ourselves.

Yvonne is a single mother with one daughter, Anthea. She lived with my grandmother in Spanish Town, Jamaica. I saw her in passing. When we came back to England she was sad. She missed our grandmother and our mother squatted on her back with all the problems of her own life and marriage. Yvonne was heart-sore, stiff-necked and exasperated. Eventually she had to leave, slamming the door behind her to go and live with Audrey. For some reason my mother disliked Yvonne. I'd use the word hate, but somehow hate is too strong a word to use when talking about a parent's feelings towards a child, even if it is more appropriate. Yvonne was the favourite of our father and any problems my mother had with him she took out on Yvonne. Just as Lance or I would receive our 'in-case' licks back in Jamaica, Yvonne took them here and she took them for all of us. Sometimes the beatings would leave the furniture stained. Yvonne was in danger and had to leave. I haven't seen Yvonne since my wedding day, not because fate is blind or the heart cold but because the world is neither hers nor mine.

Dione, the second youngest, is a care worker. She is also a single mother raising two daughters, Nisha and Ciara. I would describe Dione as an individual who is proud. She is a warm compassionate lady, very easy to get along with and thirsty for a stable life. I haven't spoken to her for over a year but I've heard she's been attacked by love's dementia, love's predicament, and now has an American to hold her. It's never too late to fall in love. We lived in a world without much of it, under a sky that never cared less. Dione's ready for a change. She holds her life in the palm of her hands but not by chance. She's not the lucky-lottery kind.

Denise, the youngest, is the single mother of one son, Lammar. She is an office worker studying accountancy. She's ambitious, focused and strong on the outside but on the inside there's a big heart. I know there's love inside, though she holds it tight. Love can hurt. We wrap and protect our heart to prevent it from bruising. One almighty blow could be enough to leave it broken. We learn from one love to the next, adding layer after layer of wrapping. Still we pick up bumps and scrapes from the things life throws at us till finally our hearts are so well packaged that we've spoiled it ourselves.

Dione and Denise are very close and will grow old together. I'll die watched over by Angela. Lance, Yvonne and Audrey? I don't know who they have. None of us can replace our one and only mother. Just as we have no choice in being born, we can't choose mothers. We fall out of them like we fall out of life to death. I had a dream that I went to visit my elder siblings many years from now. I wanted to know how life had treated them. They sat alone in their homes. I walked in and said, 'How's things?' They didn't speak, just gave me a half-smile. They didn't know me. I'd been away too long.

24

FINAL BELL . . . MAYBE

There is definitely a need for sanity and peace of mind, a need to hold precious moments by their stems. I live in hope with a fierce belief that someday we will surrender our hate and outrun our fears, but until then I will continue to stand strong, knowing that everything rests on the spilling of my light and the tearing off of my wings. I'm always careful of the black moment set by the rabbit-punch and sneaked in by the rabbit. There is a strange logic to the accelerated summer, the season of dreams. I wait for the bell in the hope that I can avoid the slow count that comes before stillness, and the darkness that closes around one's reality. The knockout is another dream, a measure of the unhurried growth of time. It's a unique place where only the mind can go after it separates itself from the body to live temporarily with forgotten moments, friends and dreams, to wander round an empty treasure trove of sound. What breaks the silence and brings illumination to sight after one shifts from life to blackness?

Once the lights have been put out the power of the mind is all that remains, a mind built within the dreams of unreal expectations. Brave kids toy dangerously with desires in a realm of fire. In the domain of dark loneliness, vulnerable fighters confront the trauma of being knocked out with a determined pride to overcome the bewildering feeling of being in a black tunnel travelling at great speed, trying to beat the count. Arriving on the other side of the tunnel we are greeted by the purest light, unbroken by counting fingers hovering detached in space.

What now for my imprisoned thoughts and their need for action? Maybe they'll reconstruct the glory of former days to bore with tales of bravery in arenas where spirit and courage seem like something vague and distant. How I loved the road I travelled to the ring, its honesty, its choking heat. The smells, the ringing bell, the screaming crowds that heighten the senses in packed stadiums are the impressions that will remain through the changing seasons. Within an aggressive hand tamed by civilised agreement there lies a magical strength. There eventually comes a time when the boxer has to step outside the circle, having been consumed by it, but the fight will not have ended. Its infinite nature will be born again by other artful hands.

I learnt something about elaborating on a vision of hope in this failing world, finally accepting that I had fallen into the dream of the living. I learnt how, with compassion, to rescue my own dream and how to sidestep the burning obstacles of memories to achieve that dream. Even though it entered the shadow of battle and even though I had to review my battle plans constantly. My head is now burning through wanting to express all those sensations I felt in and out of the ring, inside and outside of all those dissected moments when I feverishly hunted human trophies.

I'm convinced of my mortality. It's been confirmed by hands that know one truth. Life and death are real. Space and time are life's illusions. When life burns out, space and time go with it. A soul will lose itself in other souls when the coming of darkness is recognised, like a familiar chord coloured as soft as a black night filling out the background of our lives. Perhaps it will take a woman's hope to enhance the memories of this heart. After arriving exhausted, having travelled the depths of space and time, I will be born again into the clarity of her tears. The miracle of her tenderness is intimately felt in the body's centre where a rigorous clock scatters its unclouded and ordinary time in moments that crumble images into dust. Like a bottomless echo, memories will flow in and wash away festering wounds that hold on to time's ferocity. But can an ocean of time divide what is left of pain from flesh, and flesh from bone, and bone from dust?

As a silent shadow my breath was more solid than a ghost, dreaming that we're all tied to the same spirit. But how long can that dream last while inhabiting a place of blind confrontation under endless fists when only darkness listens before gradually fading with light's contact?

We are fighters tied to the common danger of hands. Like cattle we are a reminder that time has not conquered the meat market nor the slave. Defeated numbers are always neglected. The fittest men are men to whom fear is a brother they are lost without. But what if we were to be given a second chance? Or is that wishful thinking? Time swept in. A moment's hesitation changed our future. Now the moment has gone.

Thoughts for the times departed are now like distant and uncertain echoes of things that I possess but scarcely hear, so soft a melody that I hardly know for sure that they exist. They include a trainer standing as part of a team, gazing silently as his fighter staggered dispirited late in the round; tired warriors staring ahead of themselves through battered eyes between rounds; the blood that turned canvasses red and choked the donor; the nights that balanced on black shadows and slid down the eyelids like weariness down a slope. The black bottomless waters that revealed limitless lakes of time were counted by a referee. How disturbing it is to be knocked out and see that last desperate glow of light that turns dark when there's nothing left of a fight. The light instantly fades into hallucinations, which the human fear of dark imposes on space and which end so suddenly the moment a fighter realises that he has been knocked out.

A thought for the families dazzled in the cruel noise of screaming fans. The audience's delight extinguishes everything except the terrifying moments of hot and naked cranial bleeding. The dynamic moments that lead the way to tragedy and another sun on a new horizon. Then once again the obsessions of critics insincerely writing newspaper articles with fresh, sticky ink. They spin stories of brutality that everyone wants to read so as to pretend that everything today is different from what it was yesterday, reinforcing their own ignorance. Who do they think they are? Tell me their names and where they came from. Aren't they made of earth, air and water? They are more? Is that what they think and write? What makes them more? And why are they higher? What? Because they think? Have they ever seen a mind thinking? Did they enter its dark caves and explore its obstacles? Did they explore its black air and stone walls? Did their minds take them to the place where it thinks it thinks? How extraordinary or ordinary was the process of observing a mind reason? I think they think too much! Let the mind hold its mystery. The critics are no more than you or me. They were born with the rest of humanity and are made of the same substance. They are of the same origin. They are not the hidden purpose, despite the voice of vanity!

Reporters report on the complex lives that we all share, our financial difficulties, our domestic quarrels, even the thoughts which we all have to ourselves alone in our homes. Their stories are written when nobody can see them. The sexual urges and hunger of emaciated souls shake at times in absurd contradictions and outright lies. The paparazzi always seem to be the same people that live below all systems of morality, without a code of conduct, beyond the reach of ordinary people. Could a discontented reporter clean away the blood from our heads with his column without imposing a sanction on our families? To him, what do we matter?

What about the pacifists who represent the alternative to war, violence, ceaseless anger and disastrous upbringings? If only we had the freshness in our faces that comes from not having carried pain through damaged years. Without knowing me, they want me and what I represent banned. Just what is it they don't like about boxing? Didn't we consent to our own pain? Didn't they study for their own careers, picking subjects they needed for that end? Weren't they greedy for the money their jobs paid them? How can I listen to their whining? They take Caribbean holidays and whine about the sun, skiing trips and howl about the cold. Their children whine about their credit cards and computers. What terrible beginnings do they know? Do their children know anything about hunger? What about my children? I just wish they'd stop moaning, look for the positive, live and let live.

I returned to the gym under the shadows of tall buildings, back to the lessons of agonised groans and combinations of hands. I went back to the fatigue of circuit training, where strange butterflies train amid the stench of their own unwashed bodies, oblivious to the smell of stale sweat. They are obedient to the clock and to the shadows that play on rough perspiring walls. Close by, spit-buckets are filled with clots of regurgitated mucus.

Wooden steps lead up to the ring in the centre of the room surrounded by punchbags. Tracks of blood tell tales of men's dreams, forgotten until the bell awakens them to the next round of their soul's struggle with itself. After a while the sound of a bell becomes just one part of the game of ignoring pain: a pain we learnt to recognise and understand. We know its face but refuse to be in awe of it, though we sacrifice ourselves to it.

After some 25 or 30 rounds of skipping, shadow boxing, stretching and cooling down, a broken skeleton stood up under the shower wincing like a rotten tooth at the touch of cold water as it splashes on an exposed nerve. Our children played with their toys on the benches set around the outskirts of the gym walls while they waited. We are, after all, normal people, family men, though some of us hide in dark houses behind bolted doors, drawn curtains and thick walls, communicating through whispers, afraid to feel love's uncontrollable passion.

A brave kid walked straight into a right hand in front of me last week while training in the gym. He wasn't a tough kid. I never saw him with any friends or a girlfriend. He never boasted or bragged about anything. He was just an ordinary kid, sort of shy, who never did anything worth mentioning and never quite fitted in anywhere in his life. He stayed down for a while trying to hold back the tears, then he picked himself up and went home. 'His sleepless soul will perish in its pride,' I thought.

His life will not be spent in pleasant wanting. It takes more than faith. Needful things do not come unsought. Why would he expect that others should clothe and feed and, when needed, love him? By his own spirit he will be defeated. In our youth we begin by a peculiar grace from above, given something to occupy the lonely roped-off centre I now understand so well. I saw this kid in front of me unaware of the coming years. He seemed a child imbued with sense. It was as if some dire constraint of pain or rage felt by him placed more than its fair share of human weight on his young frame. What other occupation would he pursue? It's love's absence that sweeps him in, urgently standing him in the whirlwind of the seasons with their inevitable rainbows that will dance above his anguish with the tenacity and thirst of a drought. Maybe the moon will come out to play as it should, and speak without the language of hands.

The brave kid came back to the gym this week. I knew he would. I saw it in his eyes. I watched him from a distance across the small gym, although he didn't know I was looking. With a warrior-like precision he put on quite a show on the punchbag thinking that no one was watching, but hoping they were. Each move he made was firm and strong. He threw fluid combinations performed with graceful movements from side to side. His mind was focused, eyes entranced. Nothing was overbalanced or overreached. His defence looked tight while deflecting imaginary blows. His mind and body were as one. I approached the kid and asked him why he wanted to be a fighter and where he was finding his inspiration.

He told me, 'If people try to fuck with me or put me down, I want to be able to kick their fucking heads in.' He had a fighter's thoughts instilled in his head, though he couldn't see beyond his pain. He then returned the question.

I answered in an attempt to enlighten him. 'I was bound by life's duties to cut the tie that caged my expression, in order to be free. That's why I fight. I see life as it is, in colour with music and that's where I find my inspiration. But you'll never understand what pushed me or where I found the motivation to continue after dislocated shoulders, blackened eyes, fractured hands, torn muscles and broken jaws. I still took fights we believed were fought by proud men in times of peace: men's men who began their histories in arenas, dying with lions, clutching their swords without fear, fighting to be more than men. The square path to glory will be taken by you, a new generation of pugilists who'll give your hearts in hope of better lives.'

Young warriors, I wish you luck but give some thought to just what it is you're doing here and what it is you're after in this life. I was torn between responsibility to myself, duty to my family and the pull I felt towards the ring. Young fighters will one day become old enough to step back, but not old enough to give up the roar of a crowd on fight night.

The crowded spectacles in full arenas will continue to reach their climax when someone is unconscious. That may cause wonder but some things are ended with a man's darkness and, unless that darkness has a memory, will never be seen again. There will be rounds when the last eye that sees will finally close and the battered face, monstrous in defeat, will belong to me. What worthless memories will be lost in my damaged brain? The voice of love with her beautiful image will gaze into my empty corner and my mind will show itself twisted by an irreconcilable hunger. I count the night's arteries, opened with blood running free, in a growing awareness of a dream that knows better. I reflect on that inevitable pain of a physical world and weep silently in the inventive head that rests on my wife's breast. She accepts my broken body and bloodshot eyes and holds captive the heart that beats continuously in a minute-less hour. A tear may fall from the dreamer, but often beneath the surface obscure blood drowns men's hearts without sound.

In the expectant ring battered bodies are resigned to the mingling of mutual blood, running together in one merciless red flow. As if too brittle to touch, meticulously trained butterflies are overtaken by a swift darkness already placed end to end by remembered shadows. Now what words can strangle the silent destruction of physical forms? Now no tear can flatten the tidal wave of the adrenaline rush. 'This can not be allowed to happen,' critics say. I know that I don't have what they have and would have to look to a godless sky where nothing turns but an empty stomach. How could they understand unless they dreamt the same sky? Imagine it in your head: a life you don't own sealed by a fate already on the slope of drifting hope. Imagine it in your head when you go to sleep in your nice home.

Imagine blood: the blood on my shoe, nothing more than blood massed in clots on the canvas and over my arms and bruised face. Imagine the ring, the silent dialogue, broken jaws, and breath's suffocating shortage when drowning in red. Imagine breaking through pain into another zone linked with glory, respect and chopped-up dreams set free from their chains to pass through an hour. What about a face of blood that covers like thick mud and the dazzled eyes of millions searching through this thick face-pack for signs of thought with no comprehension of how that blood freezes a mind?

There will always be another ready to take my place, shaking with sleepless eyes, slurred speech and melted senses but not abandoned, with a brave heart ready to command the focus of the world, all eyes on him. I see down the corridors of memory all that got buried beneath the weight of other memories but if I go back far enough in time I come at last to me. Again I have the potential to be somebody as I once did in the beginning, when I stood alone swinging in the trenches until I bled into the dawn. Who knows defeat best? A tongue, able to taste fear in the air, signals every tendon with the twang of lightning that thrusts pulsating flesh into battle. I went forward into the cloud of fury and never looked back, not until my opponent's anger had been broken by my unchanging face and a crowd screamed for the fresh spray of blood and sweat that drops a thing of colour into time. Then they hush their throats while the furious night watches a man kiss the ground of his destiny, falling at last to an infinite season of dreams.

Life gives back scattered and unfinished chapters. Wounds are vivid in corridors of reconciled malice and the answers creep into the silent mind of an absent father. Each round remorseless eyes assert their visions in the fight's redeeming sight. Separated bodies struggle with each other's will. It seems that our minds dreamt the applause that flowed with blood's repetitive spill, but we rise from the canvas to walk beyond the ropes, finally leaving behind our severed dreams to inherit the inevitable dust.

At the start of my career I walked outside an arena with a cold breeze in my face. I knew that I would experience something beneficial so I signed on the dotted line then proceeded to mimic humanity's twisted nature. I sold my own soul to the flesh trade. I paraded isolated muscles controlled by an isolated mind. Promoters and managers worked hard to control their stables. They are the farmers and we are the cattle and here they are again, seducers of the moment, contract in one hand, pen in the other, asking me to accept new rounds, waiting to collect my minutes. Anyway, so be it. Life is what it is . . . fuck it!